THE FUTURE OF WELFARE STATE IN EAST ASIA

EDITED BY
NAOMI MIYAZATO

MYOUNG-JUNG KIM
LAN LIU
RIKIYA MATSUKURA
NAOHIRO OGAWA
SEIRITSU OGURA

YACHIYO SHUPPAN

Copyright © 2018 by Naomi Miyazato et al.

All rights reserved. No part of this publication may be reproduced or transmitted in any form or by any means, electronic or mechanical, including photocopying, recording, scanning, or any information storage or retrieval system, without written permission from the publisher.

Published by

Yachiyo Shuppan Co., Ltd.

2-2-13 Kandamisakicho Chiyoda-ku Tokyo

Phone 03-3262-0420

Fax 03-3237-0723

www.yachiyo-net.co.jp

ISBN: 978-4-8429-1715-3

First published in JAPAN on March 9, 2018

Preface

This book summarizes the results of a joint research project by the Nihon University College of Economics Center for China and Asian Studies entitled "Social Security: The Future of the Welfare State in East Asia." The development of social security and social welfare has been closely related to industrialization and modernization in the labor market. The Elizabethan Poor Law of the UK is the world's first social welfare provided by the nation. The background for the establishment of the Elizabethan Poor Law was care for farmers who, expelled from agricultural land, moved into the cities and became the poor. Germany, which industrialized rapidly, established social insurance before the Second World War. In the UK, towards the end of the war, the government published a report entitled "Social Insurance and Allied Services," also known as the Beveridge Report, which spearheaded social change in Britain. Since then advances have been mainly in Europe and the United States. Meanwhile, in Asia, social welfare development happened more slowly because of delays in industrialization. Japan advanced industrialization earlier and so faced these problems first. More recently, in Korea and Taiwan, development is progressing as industrialization does. Furthermore, China has recognized the necessity for improving social welfare to compensate for the instability of society resulting from the expansion of inequality between regions and individuals caused by rapid industrialization in recent years. The fact that industrialization and the development of social security / social welfare are closely related is common between East Asia and the West. However, East Asia is becoming an aging society with a declining birthrate far beyond the speed of population change in Europe and the United States. Just as social security and social welfare based on the pay-as-you-go system are vulnerable to the declining birthrate and the aging of the population, suppression pressure also works strongly in East Asia. On the other hand, an increase in social risks due to rapid industrialization increases the demand for social welfare.

Social security in East Asia is unique from the perspective of welfare regime theory. According to Esping-Andersen, the welfare regime of the West is roughly divided into a liberal welfare state represented by the United States, a conservative welfare state represented by the continental European countries, and a social democratic welfare state represented by Northern Europe. Although East Asian countries have similarities to conservative welfare states, families and regional communities play a more important role as suppliers of social welfare than in conservative welfare states. Therefore, the impact of the declining birthrate and aging population on social welfare is greater than in other areas.

Social security is important as social risk increases due to rapid industrialization. On the other hand, there is pressure from the public finance perspective due to the rapidly declining birthrate and aging population, and the continued reliance on family members as suppliers of social welfare. These characteristics surrounding social security in East Asia are unique. Therefore, an ideal system inevitably differs from that in the West. In this book, we investigate sustainable and efficient social security and welfare systems for the unique East Asian socio-economic climate.

Chapter 1, "Asia's Rapid Population Aging and Its Impact on the Changing Pattern of Intergenerational

Transfers" by Rikiya Matsukura and Naohiro Ogawa. In the latter half of the twentieth century, Asia's demographic landscape witnessed dramatic changes. Until the beginning of the 1980s, a number of developing countries in Asia perceived that population aging was an issue prevailing only among developed countries. However, because of their rapid fertility decline towards the end of the 20th century, coupled with their remarkable improvements in longevity, the countries of Asia have been experiencing unprecedented changes in their age structures. In some Asian countries, the child dependency ratio has been declining swiftly, generating an important demographic dividend. In other Asian countries, the rise in old age dependency has been creating formidable new policy challenges. Chapter 1 uses an analytical tool, the "National Transfer Accounts" system, and analyzes Japanese experiences of population aging and their socioeconomic impacts as a baseline for discussing important policy issues related to population aging in Asia.

Chapter 2, "The Current Status of the Earned Income Tax Credit in Korea and the Implication to Japan: Earned Income Tax Credit or Reduced Tax Rate?" by Myoung-Jung Kim. Chapter 2 investigates the effects of an Earned Income Tax Credit (EITC) that was introduced in Korea recently. On January 1, 2008, the Korean government introduced EITC to boost work incentives for the working poor by supporting the income of the tax system and achieving fair and efficient management of the social system by establishing new infrastructure. The EITC is a subsidy to support work for low earners. It aims to increase work incentives for the working poor who earn a low income or suffer from economic difficulties by providing financial incentives, which are calculated on the basis of their earned income. Currently, Japan is exploring possibilities for improvements in the function of the existing safety net. Chapter 2 considers the implications of the EITC in Japan.

Chapter 3, "Public Pension Schemes in China", by Lan Liu. Chapter 3 describes and investigates China's public pension schemes. In China, the current public pension system is mainly composed of two pillars: basic pension insurance for urban employees, and basic pension insurance for urban and rural residents. The financing resources of these two types above are different. Basic pension insurance for urban employees is financed on the basis of government, individuals and employers, whereas the financing resources of basic pension insurance for urban and rural residents includes individual contributions, collective subsidies and government subsidies. The public pension expenditures in China have increased sharply since the 1980s. Population aging has contributed to serious fiscal stresses in China, like other countries. Chapter 3 emphasizes the necessity of carrying out the further improvement of the public pension system in China.

Chapter 4, "An Empirical Analysis of the Incidence of Employers' Contributions to Health Care and Long-Term Care Insurance in Japan", by Naomi Miyazato and Seiritsu Ogura. In the last two decades, social insurance taxes for health care and long-term care in Japan have been raised repeatedly in order to finance the increasing costs of caring for the country's aging population. Almost all the laws governing social insurance programs for employed workers in Japan mandate that firms contribute at least one-half of social insurance taxes, leaving the remainder to be paid by employees. However, the employers' contributions could be shifted so that more of the burden is borne by the workers. This effect of the law on the relative tax burden of employers and employees is known as the incidence of social insurance taxes. The incidence of social insurance taxes on wages or salaries depends theoretically on the price elasticity of the demand and supply of labor. Thus, the question of how much of the past increases in social insurance taxes have shifted to labor is mainly an empirical one. Chapter 4 investigates the incidence of employers' contributions to social insurance programs with regard to both regular and non-regular workers.

Chapter 5, "Immigration Policy and Sustainability of Social Security in Japan", by Naomi Miyazato. The aging of the population in Japan is the most severe among all developed countries. Before the baby-boomer generation started to retire, Japan's government proposed and implemented many social security reforms. Unfortunately, it is hard to say if those reforms will achieve sustainability of Japan's social security system. There are only two ways for sound financing of social security: decreasing benefit levels or increasing tax revenues. Although analyzing and debating the recovery of the birthrate have often been discussed for increasing tax revenues, immigration policy has barely been investigated, despite the strong implication for the sustainability of social security. Chapter 5 investigates whether an immigration policy could mitigate intergenerational imbalances and achieve sustainability of the social security system in Japan by using a dynamic general equilibrium simulation model.

We would like to express our deep gratitude to all participants who made presentations and provided comments at the conference, and the Nihon University College of Economics Center for China and Asian Studies that provided research funding for this project.

Contributors

Myoung-Jung Kim   NLI Research Institute, Tokyo, Japan   Chapter 2

Lan Liu   Peking University, Peking, China   Chapter 3

Rikiya Matsukura   Nihon University, Tokyo, Japan   Chapter 1

Naomi Miyazato   Nihon University, Tokyo, Japan   Chapter 4, Chapter 5

Naohiro Ogawa   Nihon University, Tokyo, Japan   Chapter 1

Seiritsu Ogura   Hosei University, Tokyo, Japan   Chapter 4

Contents

Preface   *i*

Chapter 1
**Asia's Rapid Population Aging and Its Impact on
the Changing Pattern of Intergenerational Transfers** ———————— *1*

   1   Introduction   *1*
   2   The System of the National Transfer Accounts: What Can It Do?   *2*
   3   Factors Underlying Family and Public Support Systems in Asia   *4*
     3.1   Limits to the Family Support System and Value Shifts   *4*
     3.2   Public Support System and Economic Development   *8*
   4   First and Second Demographic Dividends   *11*
   5   Lifecycle Deficits and Lifecycle Reallocations   *17*
   6   Concluding Remarks   *24*

Chapter 2
**The Current Status of the Earned Income Tax Credit in Korea
and the Implication to Japan: Earned Income Tax Credit or Reduced Tax Rate?** ———————— *27*

   1   Introduction   *27*
   2   Background and Process of the Introduction of the EITC in South Korea   *27*
   3   Process and Overview of South Korean EITC   *31*
     3.1   Process and Changes of the EITC   *31*
     3.2   Purpose of the EITC   *32*
     3.3   Application Process of the EITC and Standard of Application   *33*
     3.4   EITC Payment System and Current Situation for Payment   *35*
     3.5   Extension of Coverage of the EITC and the CTC to the Self-Employed   *37*
   4   Analysis on Effects and Challenges Ahead   *38*
   5   Implication to Japan   *42*

Chapter 3
Public Pension Schemes in China ———————————————— *45*

   1   Introduction   *45*
   2   Background   *45*
     2.1   Population Aging   *45*
     2.2   Reform Progress of Public Pension System   *47*
   3   Public Pension Arrangements   *49*
     3.1   Basic Pension Insurance for Urban Employees   *50*
     3.2   Basic Pension Insurance for Urban and Rural Residents   *52*
   4   Features of Public Pension System   *54*
     4.1   SP & IRA and PAYG   *54*
     4.2   Financing Responsibility of the Government   *54*
     4.3   "Real Account" of Basic Pension Insurance for Urban and Rural Residents   *55*

4.4　Diversity of Basic Pension Insurance for Urban and Rural Residents　*56*

5　Reform of Public Pension System　*56*

5.1　Extending Retirement Ages　*57*

5.2　Eliminating Transfer Costs　*57*

5.3　Reducing Average Replacement Rates　*57*

5.4　Expanding the Coverage of Public Pension Insurance System　*58*

5.5　Setting Up Independent Accounts　*58*

5.6　Guaranteeing Financing Resources　*59*

5.7　Promoting Integration of Urban-Rural System　*59*

5.8　Promoting Transfer and Integration of Different Systems　*59*

Chapter 4

An Empirical Analysis of the Incidence of Employers' Contributions to Health Care and Long-Term Care Insurance in Japan ——————— *61*

1　Introduction　*61*

2　Preceding Studies　*62*

3　Institutional Backgrounds　*63*

4　Estimation Model and Data　*65*

4.1　Estimation Model　*65*

4.2　Data and Descriptive Statistics　*66*

5　Estimation Results　*69*

6　Concluding Remarks　*74*

Chapter 5

Immigration Policy and Sustainability of Social Security in Japan ——————— *77*

1　Introduction　*77*

2　The model　*78*

2.1　Demographic Structure and Immigration Policies　*78*

2.2　Households　*80*

2.3　The Government　*81*

2.4　Firms and Technology　*82*

3　Simulation Analysis　*82*

3.1　Specification of the Parameters　*82*

3.2　Simulation Results　*83*

4　Concluding Remarks　*86*

Index　*88*

Chapter 1

Asia's Rapid Population Aging and Its Impact on the Changing Pattern of Intergenerational Transfers

Rikiya Matsukura and Naohiro Ogawa

1 Introduction

In the latter half of the twentieth century, Asia's demographic landscape witnessed dramatic changes. Until the beginning of the 1980s, a number of developing countries in Asia perceived that population aging was an issue prevailing only among developed countries. However, as a consequence of their rapid fertility decline toward the end of the 20th century, coupled with their remarkable improvements in longevity, the countries of Asia have been experiencing unprecedented changes in their age structures. In some Asian countries, the child dependency ratio has been declining swiftly, generating an important demographic dividend. In other Asian countries, the rise in old age dependency has been creating formidable new policy challenges. It should be stressed that the policy response to these changes will obviously influence economic growth and poverty, intergenerational equity, and social welfare for many decades to come.

Primarily because the fertility transition in many Asian countries, particularly in East and Southeast Asia, has been substantially shorter than in the developed countries, the speed of population aging in Asia has been and will be much faster than that observed among the industrialized nations in Europe (United Nations, 2002). In Asia, Japan's fertility decline was the earliest to occur. In addition, it was also the greatest in magnitude among all the industrialized nations. By and large, the current demographic picture in Japan is similar to that of Europe.

European fertility has been below replacement level for the region as a whole for almost four decades, suggesting that this below-replacement fertility phenomenon is neither temporary nor transitory (Lesthaeghe and Willems, 1999). As a result, there is a rapidly growing sentiment among European demographers that below-replacement fertility is a persistent long-term trend (Sinding, 2002). This view pertaining to Europe's future fertility levels has been part of the United Nations population projections since 1998.

Peter McDonald (2005) divided industrialized countries in Europe into two groups in terms of their fertility levels. Group 1 consists of all the Nordic countries, all the English-speaking countries, and the French and Dutch speaking countries in Western Europe. In these countries, TFR is above 1.5 births per woman. Group 2 countries, with TFR below 1.5, consist of all the South European countries, and all the German-speaking countries of Western Europe. All the industrialized East Asian countries can be categorized in Group 2, although they are outside Europe. Moreover, fertility is now lowest in East Asia in the entire world. It is also interesting to observe that Group 2 countries have a strong traditional value relating to familial responsibilities so that families play a principal role in supporting their own members without relying on heavy support from the state.

It is axiomatic among demographers that declining fertility, not increased life expectancy, is the principal determinant of population aging at its early stage. It should be stressed, however, that the mortality effect on population aging becomes increasingly strong as the process of demographic transition and economic development progresses (United Nations, 1987). At present, the mortality effect on population aging seems relatively limited in most of the Asian countries, as compared with the fertility effect. However, if the recent trends in mortality improvement continue in these countries, mortality at advanced ages will fall substantially in the relatively near future, thus contributing to population aging as a major factor. It is generally considered that the role of mortality improvements in inducing the aging process becomes increasingly important over time, especially when life expectancy at birth exceeds 70 years (Myers, 1988). In many of the industrialized nations in Europe, life expectancy at birth for both sexes combined has been quickly approaching 80 years, and some of the developing Asian countries have already achieved a higher than 70-year life expectancy at birth. One can easily conceive that in both Europe and Asia, the mortality effect will overtake the fertility effect in the not so distant future.

At present, Japan's population aging level is by far the highest in Asia. Moreover, in 2005, the population of Japan became the oldest national population in the world, surpassing the Italian population (Ogawa, 2005). In view of Japan's traditional family organization and traditional cultural values prevailing in Asia, the present paper will heavily draw upon Japanese experiences of population aging and their socioeconomic impacts as a baseline for discussing important policy issues related to population aging in Asia. To achieve this objective, we will utilize, as an analytical tool, the "National Transfer Accounts" system, which will be succinctly described in the following section.

2   The System of the National Transfer Accounts: What Can It Do?

In the recent past, an international collaborative research project has been implemented under the leadership of the East-West Center (Andrew Mason) and the Center for the Economics and Demography of Aging at the University of California, Berkeley (Ronald Lee). As of March 2016, there are 48 countries participating in this international collaborative project.

One of the primary objectives of this project is to develop the National Transfer Accounts (NTA), which is a system for measuring economic flows across age groups. These flows arise because in any viable society, dependent members of the population - those who consume more than they produce - are supported by members of the population who produce more than they consume. Societies take different approaches to reallocating resources from surplus to deficit ages, but two methods dominate. One method relies on capital markets. Individuals accumulate capital during their working ages. When they are no longer productive, the elderly can support their consumption by relying on capital income (interest, dividends, rental income, profits, etc.) and by liquidating their assets. The second method relies on transfers from those at surplus ages to those at deficit ages. Some transfers are mediated by the public sector.

Important examples are public education, publicly financed healthcare, and public pension programs. Many transfers are private transfers of which familial transfers are most important. The material needs of children are provided mostly by their parents. In Asian societies familial transfers between adult children and the elderly are also very important. Some of these transfers are between households, but intra-household transfers are much more important. Family members form multi-generation households that involve substantial intergenerational transfers.

National Transfer Accounts provide a comprehensive framework for estimating consumption, production, and resource reallocations by age. The accounts are constructed so as to be consistent with and complementary to National Income and Product Accounts (NIPA). The accounts are being constructed with sufficient historical depth to allow for analysis of key features of the transfer system. Sectoral disaggregation allows the analysis of public and private education and healthcare spending. The accounts can also be projected to analyze the economic and policy implications of future demographic changes.

The NTA system will provide important new information relevant to the following issues:

(i) *Intergenerational Equity and Poverty*. How resources are shared across generations is one of the most important determinants of equity and poverty. Children and the elderly are most vulnerable because their responses to economic hardship are so limited. The NTA system measures how consumption varies across generations and will allow for international comparisons currently not possible;

(ii) *Aging Policy*. Many Asian countries face the prospect of rapid population aging. They are developing new programs and considering reforms of old programs intended to meet vital needs of the elderly without undue sacrifice on the part of other generations now and in the future. The NTA system will provide the information base needed to evaluate alternative policies, to assess their effects on intergenerational equity, and their implications for economic growth;

(iii) *The First Demographic Dividend*. The first demographic dividend arises because changes in population age structure have led to an increase in the working ages relative to the non-working ages. To be more precise the first demographic dividend arises because of an increase in the share of the population at ages during which production exceeds consumption;

(iv) *The Second Demographic Dividend*. The second demographic dividend arises in response to the prospect of population aging. In countries that rely on capital accumulation to meet the retirement needs of the elderly, population aging provides a powerful incentive to accumulate wealth. This phenomenon has been important to the economic success of East Asia's high-performing economies. In countries that rely on transfers to meet the retirement needs of the elderly, the second demographic dividend may not emerge; and

(v) *Childbearing Incentives*. Countries vary with respect to the cost of children and the extent to which those costs are borne by parents. The NTA system provides estimates of the cost of children and the extent to which those costs are subsidized by the public sector. This information may be useful for understanding why high fertility persists in some countries and why very low fertility persists in others.

In the present paper, we will analyze some of these issues by presenting some of the preliminary findings recently produced by the NTA project. The issues which this paper deals with include first and second demographic dividends, and a changing pattern of consumption among generations. In the ensuing section, to facilitate our discussions on these issues, we will pay attention (1) to a changing pattern of living arrangements among the elderly, which provides a base for familial transfers and (2) to the current profile of the social security system, which plays a crucial role in facilitating public transfers.

3 Factors Underlying Family and Public Support Systems in Asia

It is generally considered that although family-based support systems provide a principal source of old-age security at early stages of economic development, the responsibility for taking care of aged dependants is gradually shifted to the public support system as the developmental process continues (Ogawa, 1992; Ogawa and Retherford, 1997).

3.1 Limits to the Family Support System and Value Shifts

As has been widely documented (Treas and Logue, 1986), levels and the nature of family support vary substantially with the level of economic development. In most developing countries such as those in Asia, numerous support services for the elderly are provided by families. In developed countries, however, public transfers play a significant role in supporting the elderly, although families still provide their elderly dependants with many support services.

One of the most salient factors contributing to this difference between developing and developed nations is the pronounced difference in family structure between them. Traditional extended families are still prevalent in developing Asia. According to an international comparative survey on the elderly undertaken in 1996 (Management and Coordination Agency, 1997), the proportion of the elderly at ages 60 and over living in three-generational households was 42.6% in Thailand, 35.5% in the Republic of Korea, and 29.1% in Japan. In contrast, in the case of the United States and Germany, it was 1.8% each. In addition, the proportion of the elderly coresiding with their children has been on a downward trend over the last two decades in the three Asian countries under consideration, as displayed in Figure 1-1. In Japan, the proportion of the elderly aged 60 and over coresiding with an adult child declined from 36.9 in 1981 to 22.0% in 2001. In the case of the Republic of Korea, it decreased from 38.1% in 1991 to 26.3% in 2001. In Thailand, it fell from 48.5% in 1986 to 42.6% in 1996.

Using micro-level data gathered in many Asian countries as part of the Demographic and Health Household Survey, Bongaarts and Zimmer (2001) asserts that the association between older adults' schooling and living arrangement patterns tends to substantiate the hypothesis that older adults living in developing countries with high scores for socioeconomic indicators are less likely to be living in extended families. This view seems to be in agreement with Goode's convergence theory (1963), suggesting that there exists a movement toward family nuclearization and a weakening of the extended family system as socioeconomic development advances.

In an ASEAN aging survey conducted in the mid-1980s (Jones, 1988), respondents aged 60 years and

Chapter 1   Asia's Rapid Population Aging and Its Impact on the Changing Pattern of Intergenerational Transfer   5

Figure 1-1. Changes in the Proportion of 60+ Who are Living in Three-Generational Households, Selected Countries, 1981-2001

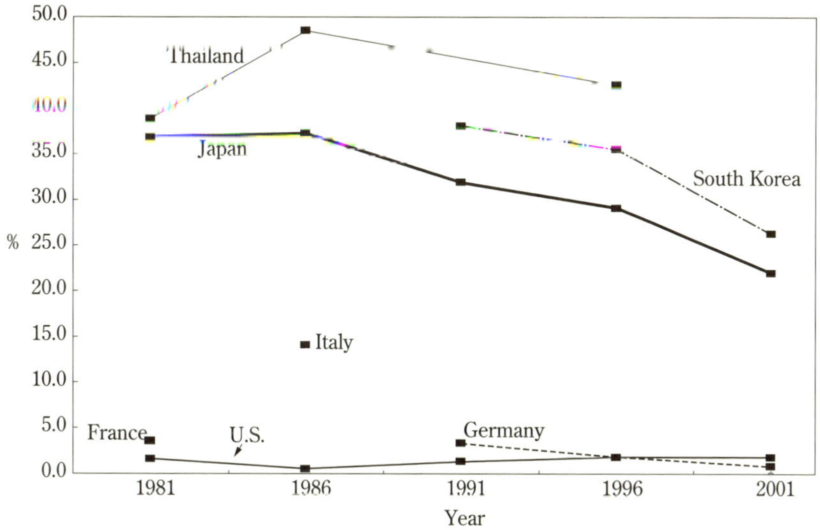

Source: Management and Coordination Agency (various years) *Brief Summary of the International Comparative Survey of the Elderly*, Tokyo: Gyosei Printing Co.

Table 1-1. Income Sources for the Elderly Aged 60 and Older in Selected Countries, 1996

Specific income source	Percent responding that specific source is main source				
	Japan	United States	South Korea	Germany	Thailand
Work	21.6	15.5	26.6	4.6	27.0
Public pensions	57.1	55.5	2.9	77.0	7.3
Private pensions	1.7	13.3	0.5	10.1	2.1
Savings	2.4	1.5	4.9	1.6	1.9
Assets	2.5	8.5	4.5	2.0	4.8
Children	4.2	0.0	56.3	0.2	52.9
Public assistance	0.3	0.3	3.7	1.7	0.3
Other	2.4	1.6	0.3	2.2	3.6
No answer	7.9	3.7	0.4	0.0	0.3

Source: Management and Coordination Agency (various years) *Brief Summary of the International Comparative Survey of the Elderly*, Tokyo: Gyosei Printing Co.

over were asked what their main source of old-age support was. The collected data show that the pattern differed by country to a certain extent, and varied by sex to a greater extent. In Singapore, Malaysia, Thailand, and Indonesia, families were the principal source of monetary and material support for a large majority of aged women. Children and grandchildren were also a major source of income for elderly men, but family support was considerably less important for men than for women. Instead, income from their own economic activity was more important for men than for women.

The picture of the family support system that emerged from the ASEAN aging survey seems to be still largely valid in Asia, according to the international comparative survey undertaken in 1996 (Management and Coordination Agency, 1997). Data presented in Table 1-1 indicate that in both Thailand and the Republic of Korea more than half of the elderly aged 60 and over relied on their children as their main income source in the mid-1990s. In contrast, the proportion of the elderly whose main income source was public pensions was only 2.9% in the Republic of Korea and 7.3% in Thailand.

Another vital source of income for old persons in Asian countries is their own economic activity, as has been demonstrated in many previous studies (Ogawa et al., 2005). Furthermore, data on the income sources collected in the 1996 international comparative survey show that approximately one-third of the elderly in Thailand and the Republic of Korea worked to make a living. In an agricultural society like Thailand, these results are highly conceivable. It is generally considered that the high labor force participation rates for the aged in agricultural societies represent the relatively strong economic position of old people. One important factor underlying this view is that the economic value of knowledge and experience relative to physical prowess is generally high in agriculture.

These cross-sectional results are supported by time-series data for Japan, gathered in a series of nationwide surveys concerning fertility and family planning, which have been carried out every other year since 1950 by Mainichi Newspapers (Population Problems Research Council, 2004). Since the first round of the survey, with the exception of a few rounds, the question regarding the dependence on children for old-age security has been asked of married women of reproductive age who have at least one child. The recoded responses were as follows: (i) "expect to depend," (ii) "do not expect," and (iii) "never thought about it." Figure 1-2 shows intertemporal changes over the period 1950-2004 in the percentage of the respondents who chose the category, "expect to depend." The proportion of respondents who expect to depend on their own children declined almost continuously over the period in question. Almost two-thirds of Japanese married women in 1950 expressed an expectation to depend on their own children, but only 10.9% in 2000 intended to depend on their own children for old-age security.

Since 1963, the question on the attitude of wives toward taking care of aged parents has been asked in the successive rounds of the Mainichi Newspapers' surveys. The precoded response categories are as follows: (i) "good custom," (ii) "natural duty as children," (iii) "unavoidable due to inadequacy of public support resources," and (iv) "not a good custom." Figure 1-2 presents changes in the percentage of those who chose one of the first two response categories: (i) "good custom" and (ii) "natural duty as

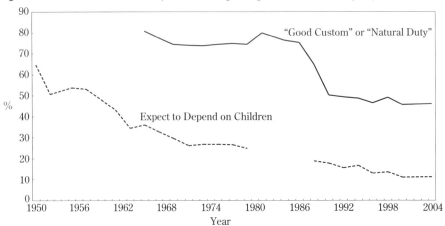

Figure 1-2. Trends in Norms and Expectations Regarding Care for the Elderly: Japan, 1950-2004

Source: Mainichi Newspapers of Japan (various years) *National Survey on Family Planning*.
Mainichi Newspapers of Japan (2004) *The first round of the National Survey on Population, Families and Generations*.

children." The plotted results indicate that the proportion of respondents who felt that providing care for elderly parents was either a good custom or natural duty had been, by and large, stable over the period 1963-1986. From 1986 to 1988, however, the percentage distribution changed dramatically, and the declining trend is still under way.

The results set out in Figure 1-2 indicate that in the process of Japanese postwar economic development, children›s utility as old-age security for their parents has decreased considerably, and family support provided by married women for elderly parents has also declined. Moreover, a further in-depth statistical analysis of the time-series data has shown that the recent trends in both the attitudes of Japanese married women toward aged parents and their dependence on children for old-age security are likely to continue in the years to come, but this scenario is likely to be seriously affected depending on how social security policies such as old-age pensions and medical care programs are formulated by the government (Ogawa and Retherford, 1993a, 1993b ; Retherford et al., 1999).

In addition to the shift of values related to intergenerational relationships, the demographic availability of adult children for the provision of care for aged parents changes as the process of population aging advances. To measure the demands on families (at ages 50-64) to provide support for their oldest-old members (aged 85 and over), the parent support ratio has been commonly used in the recent past (United Nations, 2002). This ratio relates the oldest-old to their presumed offspring, who were born when the older persons were in their 20s and 30s. In 2000, the parent support ratio for Asia as a whole is 2.6 persons over 85 years per hundred persons aged 50-64, but it is projected to rise to 10.0 persons in 2050. Particularly, the magnitude of growth in the parent support ratio is phenomenal in East Asia. It will grow from 3.3 persons in 2000 to 17.2 persons in 2050. Another indicator is the familial support ratio which represents the demands on women at ages 40-59 to give care to their aged parents (65-84). In Asia as a whole, it was 1.87 persons in 2000, but is expected to decline to 1.05 persons in 2050.

These shifts in the numerical relationship between aged parents and their adult children in Asia seem to indicate that the durability of traditional patterns of family care for the aged by adult children will be increasingly questioned with the passage of time. This implies that as the aging process proceeds in Asian countries, an increasing number of these countries are likely to replace the family support system with the public support system. However, the large inter-country differences in the demographic availability of the intergenerational support system among the Asian countries suggest that the timing to shift policy emphasis from the family support system to the public support system should vary considerably from country to country in the years to come. In addition, the extent to which the governments shift their policy emphasis from family support to public support depends heavily on the pace and magnitude of the deterioration of the potential support ratio in their future developmental processes. Besides these demographic factors, a variety of elements need to be considered in formulating such long-term macroeconomic plans for the emerging aging societies in Asia, as will be discussed in the ensuing section.

3.2 Public Support System and Economic Development

Data shown in Figure 1-3, which cover both European and Asian countries in 1996/1997, point to an increase in the importance of public pension programs as economic development proceeds. This graphical exposition shows that the share of GDP allocated to the provision of old-age pension benefits rises with per capita GNP measured in US dollars in both Europe (34 countries) and Asia (17 countries). It is worth reporting that the regression line for each region shows that the Asian countries show a greater variance with a lower goodness of fit ($R^2=0.26$) than their European counterparts ($R^2=0.63$). There are, however, various data limitations with regard to the provision of social security benefits. Also, although the correlation between the two variables is considerably high, Figure 1-3 indicates that there are substantial differences among different countries even when their levels of economic development are comparable. This implies that the compositional shift of support resources for the elderly over the course of economic development is subject to a host of non-economic factors that are demographic, sociocultural, ideological, and historical. For those reasons, the pattern emerging from the above inter-country data should be interpreted cautiously.

The clustering of observations in Figure 1-3, particularly for the developing countries in Asia at an initial stage of economic development, is attributable mainly to the fact that pension programs in these countries are limited in terms of duration, size, and coverage. According to data published by the United

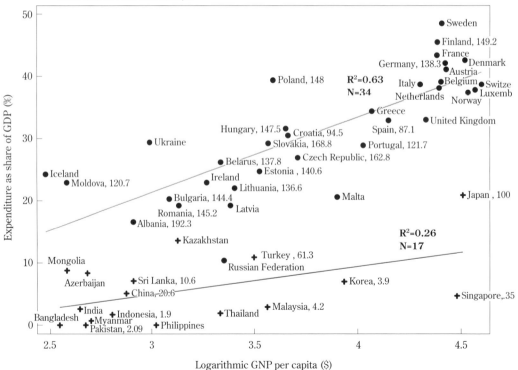

Figure 1-3. Relationship Between Economic Development and Share of GDP Allocated to Pension Benefits in 1996/1997 in Asia and Europe

Source: ILO (2000) *World Labour Report*.

States Social Security Administration and covering 26 ESCAP member countries, old-age security programs had been introduced in only six member countries before 1950. This is what one would expect, because most developing nations are short of economic resources and such programs are difficult to administer.

Besides old-age pensions, health care services constitute the core of the social security system in most countries, both Asia and Europe. As has been the case with the old-age pension programs, data plotted in Figure 1-4, covering both European and Asian countries in 1996/1997, indicate an increase in the share of the public medical programs in GDP as economic development proceeds. As compared with the case of old-age pension programs, the share of GDP allocated to the provision of medical care services grows with per capita GNP in both Europe (34 countries) and Asia (17 countries), although the variance is considerably larger in medical care programs than in old-age pension programs.

It is generally believed that health care is more widely available to the elderly in the majority of developing countries than pensions. This is certainly the case in Asia's developing countries (Martin, 1988). However, the adequacy and accessibility of health care differs by country as well as within each country. In China, for example, the urban elderly retired from state-owned enterprises receive free medical care services, whereas the medical care costs for all other urban elderly are covered by municipal governments. In Singapore, a part of each persons account in the Central Provident Fund has been used for the Medisave program since 1984. In Malaysia, comprehensive health and medical services are

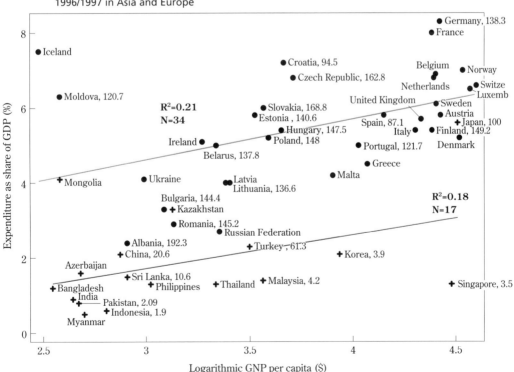

Figure 1-4. Relationship Between Economic Development and Share of GDP Allocated to Health Care in 1996/1997 in Asia and Europe

Source: ILO (2000) *World Labour Report*.

available to the general population, but not specifically for the elderly (Ogawa, 1988).

In Thailand, a major change was introduced into its medical care plan in 2001. It is called the "30 Baht Health Care Scheme," by which patients pay only 30 baht per visit to a medical facility, with additional costs covered by the government (Kamnuansilpa and Wongthanavasu, 2002). Because of its low price, this new scheme can be regarded as a virtually universal medical care plan. Prior to the new plan, only limited segments of the population were covered by medical insurance schemes, one of which was the "health card" plan. The purpose of the health card scheme was to provide health care security to those who were not covered by any other health scheme. One health card covered card holders and their families not exceeding five persons, and the benefits included free medical care, necessary preventive care, and rehabilitation services by a registered provider. The cost of providing such benefits was estimated at 1,000 baht per card, but card holders paid only 500 baht, and the remaining 500 baht was subsidized by the government (Phananiramai and McCleary, 1998).

Because of the high cost of hospital use and technology in caring for an ever-increasing elderly population, growing attention has been directed toward the role of families in supporting the health of their aged parents in both developing and developed countries. In Japan, families are likely to face an extremely fast growth in the number of aged parents who need intensive care at home. These elderly parents in need of such care include those suffering from senile dementia and those who are bedridden. Owing to the wide prevalence of extended families and the limited availability of institutional care, the majority of these aged persons are looked after at home in contemporary Japanese society. More importantly, it is middle-aged women outside the labor force who usually assume this responsibility. In view of this, the ratio of non-working women at various ages, compared with the bedridden or senile elderly persons, has been projected over the period 2000-2025, as shown in Figure 1-5. As can be inspected from this graph, the probability for full-time housewives at ages 40-49 taking care of these elderly patients rises from approximately 14% in 2000 to 45% in 2025.

In an aging society like Japan, however, it is conceivable that owing to a growing scarcity of the overall labor supply, labor demand placed on the women of this age group would increase gradually. For this reason, the availability of institutional care as an alternative to home care should be urgently expanded to alleviate the heavy burden on these middle-aged women taking care of elderly patients. It should be borne in mind, however, that the provision of such care in institutions gives rise not only to higher health care costs but also to the deterioration of the psychological and emotional well-being of the sick elderly. In view of these negative consequences, the government of Japan implemented its Long-term Care Insurance Scheme in 2000 in hope of facilitating in-home care. However, the demand for services under this scheme has been growing at an unexpectedly rapid rate, leading the government to drastically change the criteria for providing its services in April 2006 and in subsequent years.

It is worth remarking that there are two major differences between old-age pension schemes and health care programs in terms of financing. First, most of the old-age pensions currently available in developing countries involve a certain degree of intergenerational transfers from the young to the old, while health care services can be regarded as transfers from the healthy to the unhealthy. This implies

Chapter 1 Asia's Rapid Population Aging and Its Impact on the Changing Pattern of Intergenerational Transfer

Figure 1-5. Projected Ratio of the Elderly Population Who Suffer from Senile Dementia or Who are Bedridden to the Nonworking Population at Various Ages, Japan 2000-2025

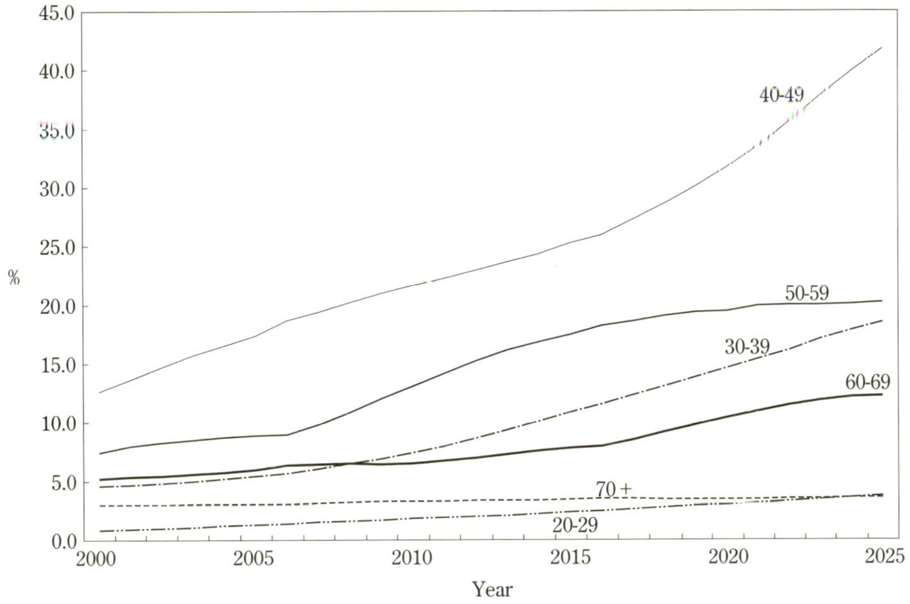

Source: Calculated by the authors using the NUPRI long-term macroeconomic-demographic-social security model.

that change in the social security system is likely to affect different segments of the population differently, depending on whether change is related to a pension component or a health service component. Second, pensions usually require each participant to make contributions for many years before benefits are paid, but in health care each individual is entitled to receive medical care services as soon as he or she is enrolled in the program. For this reason, where there is less economic development, the cost of health care–rather than pensions–tends to be the major financing problem in the social security system.

By and large, the discussion so far indicates a shift in responsibility for providing economic security to the elderly from the family to the state as societies develop. However, there are many similarities and equally many dissimilarities in the pattern of provision of support resources, not only between countries at different levels of economic development, but also between those at comparable levels. It is important to note that falling fertility, which contributes to making a population age, generates economic gains. Depending upon how the gains are utilized in the course of economic development, the future well-being of the elderly will be seriously affected.

4 First and Second Demographic Dividends

As has been recently discussed extensively elsewhere (Mason, 2001, 2005 ; Mason and Lee, 2006), one of the important linkages between demographic transformations and economic growth is the role of demographic dividends in the process of economic development. As a country advances along the stages of demographic transition, it undergoes considerable age structural shifts. When the country's fertility begins to fall, the first demographic dividend arises because changes in population age structure have led to an increase in the working ages relative to non-working ages. In other words, the first demographic dividend arises because of an increase in the share of the population at ages during which production exceeds consumption. That is, the first demographic dividend is positive when the rate of growth in output per effective consumer exceeds the rate of growth in output per effective producer (Mason, 2005).

To illustrate first and second demographic dividends, let us use the case of Japan. With a view to calculating the first demographic dividend, we have estimated the age-specific profiles of consumption with both private and public sectors combined and those of production in contemporary Japan. The estimated results are presented in Figure 1-6. These profiles have been depicted, by drawing upon private-sector information derived from the *National Survey of Family Income and Expenditure* (NSFIE) for 1999 carried out by the Statistics Bureau of Japan, and public-sector information for 1999 gleaned from various government publications. By applying the computed age-specific results displayed in this graphical exposition as statistical weights to adjust the entire population over the period 1920-2040, we have calculated the annual growth rate of output per effective consumer and the annual growth rate of output per effective producer over the period 1920-2040. Regarding the population for the period beyond 2000, we have utilized the population projection prepared by the Nihon University Population Research Institute (hereafter, "NUPRI population projection"). As the detailed description of the NUPRI population projection has been provided elsewhere (Ogawa et al., 2003), no further discussion pertaining to the derivation of the projection will be given here. The computed results are shown in Figure 1-7.

A brief glance at the computed results illustrated in Figure 1-7 reveals that Japan's first demographic dividend, which corresponds to the difference between the annual growth rate of output per effective consumer and the annual growth rate of output per effective producer, had been positive for 46 years from 1949 to 1995, except for 1980. But the magnitude of the positive first demographic dividend was

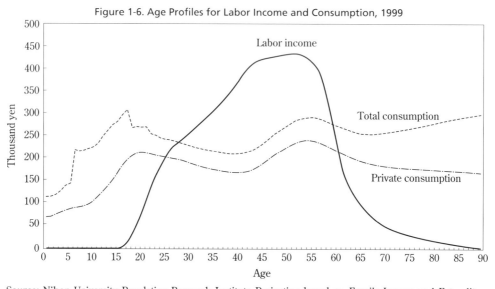

Figure 1-6. Age Profiles for Labor Income and Consumption, 1999

Source: Nihon University Population Research Institute Projection based on *Family Income and Expenditure Survey* (1999), Statistics Bureau, Ministry of Internal Affairs and Communications, Japan.

extremely large during the rapid economic growth of the 1960s and the early 1970s, as presented in Figure 1-8.

As has been the case with postwar Japan, the first demographic dividend typically lasts for a few decades, but it is inherently transitory in nature. The same demographic forces that produce an end to the first dividend lead to a second demographic dividend. That is, in the process of age structural transformations, the second demographic dividend arises in response to the prospect of population aging. For instance, in countries that rely on capital accumulation to meet the retirement needs of the elderly, population aging provides a powerful incentive to accumulate wealth. It is important to note, however,

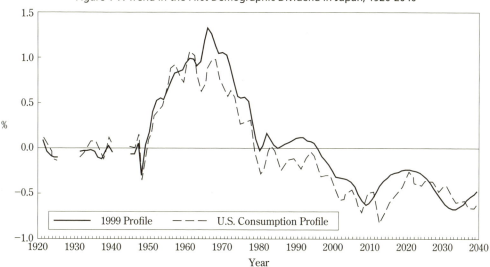

Figure 1-7. Trend in the First Demographic Dividend in Japan, 1920-2040

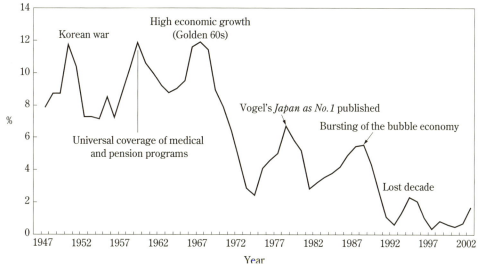

Figure 1-8. Trend in Real GDP Growth Rate: Japan, 1948-2003

Note: Three-year moving average.
Source: Economic and Social Research Institute, Cabinet Office, Government of Japan (various years) *Annual Report on National Accounts*.

that in countries that rely on transfers, both public and familial, in meeting the retirement needs of the elderly, the second demographic dividend may not emerge. While the first dividend is purely accounting-oriented, the second dividend consists of both compositional and behavioral effects (Mason, 2005 ; Ogawa and Matsukura, 2005). The second dividend is affected not only by the numbers of the elderly persons relative to younger persons, but also by the extent to which consumers and policy makers are forward-looking and respond effectively to the demographic changes that are anticipated in the years ahead. When life expectancy is increasing, for example, the impetus for accumulating wealth is stimulated, which, in turn, leads to a permanent increase in income. This implies that if capital accumulation rather than familial or public transfer programs dominate the age reallocation systems for supporting the elderly, population aging may yield a second demographic dividend in the form of higher rates of saving and capital intensification of the economy (Mason, 2005).

Compared with the first dividend, measuring the amount of the second dividend is considerably more difficult, in part because the accumulation of wealth is intrinsically forward looking. In the present study, as has been the case with previous studies (Mason, 2005), we have simplified the computational procedure by making the following two major assumptions. First, we have assumed that the growth rates of the capital and lifecycle wealth are equal, and the elasticity of labor income, with respect to capital, is set equal to 0.5. Second, we have assumed that the wealth held by those aged 50 and older is closely connected with the effect of demography on lifecycle wealth and the second demographic dividend. It should be also noted that the population for the period 2000-2050 has been estimated by extending NUPRI's population projection period beyond 2025.

As asserted by Mason (2005), the second demographic dividend is computed as the growth rate of the wealth-income ratio, which corresponds to 0.5 times the difference between (i) the present value of future lifetime consumption of all persons at a certain cut-off age (50 years old in this exercise) or earlier per effective consumer in year t and (ii) the present value of future production of all persons at the cut-off age or earlier per effective producer in year t.

The estimates of the second demographic dividend over the period 1950-2030 are shown in Figure 1-9. A few points of interest emerge from Figure 1-9. First of all, Japan's second demographic dividend is negative up 1958. Apparently, this result reflects the fact that the Japanese economy had been seriously destroyed during World War II and was still in shambles for the most part of the 1950s. Second, Japan's second demographic dividend increases remarkably in the 1960s and 1970s, and remains at a considerably high level for the latter half of the twentieth century. One salient example of the rapid increase in wealth in the early 1960s was the establishment of the universal pension plans, and their reserved funds have accumulated at a phenomenal rate, as shown in,. Third, beginning from the 1990s, the amount of the second demographic dividend fluctuates to a considerable extent, with a pronounced trough in the 2010s, followed by a substantial upsurge in the 2020s and 2030s. These oscillations are substantially attributable to the rapid age compositional shifts in the early part of the twenty-first century, primarily because the second generation of baby boomers enter the age group 50 years old and over.

These computational results pertaining to both first and second demographic dividends in Japan

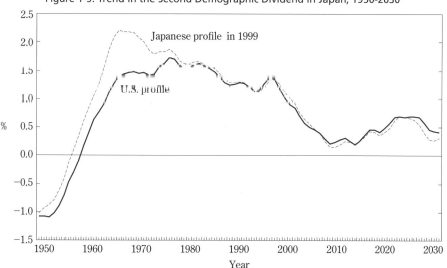

Figure 1-9. Trend in the Second Demographic Dividend in Japan, 1950-2030

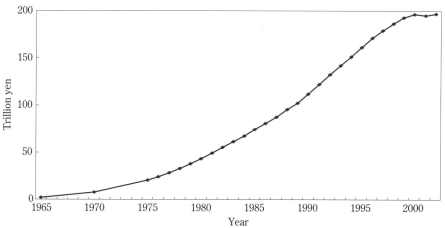

Figure 1-10. Growth of Reserved Funds for All Public Pension Schemes Combined, 1965-2002

Source: Ministry of Health, Labour and Welfare (2003, 2004) *Financial Report on the Public Pension System: Fiscal Year*.

provide an additional piece of empirical evidence, pointing to the high likelihood that the unprecedented fertility reduction subsequent to the baby boom (1947-1949) played an important role in boosting the growth of per capita income at a phenomenal rate during this high economic growth period. As presented in Table 1-2, among the five time periods under question, a sum of the first and second demographic dividends was the largest during the rapid economic growth. In contrast, they were miniscule in both the 1950s and 1980s. It is also interesting to note that in the first half of the 1990s, the second demographic dividend was considerably large as a result of inflated wealth caused by the "bubble economy" from the mid-1980s to the early 1990s.

By applying the age profiles of consumption and labor income for the United States in 2000 to the United Nations' population projection for a number of countries, Mason (2005) computed the timing of

Table 1-2. Estimates of the First and Second Dividends, Actual Growth in GDP per Effective Consumer, 1950-1995, Japan

Time period	Demographic dividends			Actual growth in GDP per effective consumer	Actual dividend
	First	Second	Total		
1950-1960	0.61	−0.49	0.13	7.00	6.87
1960-1970	1.07	1.67	2.74	10.55	7.81
1970-1980	0.64	1.89	2.53	12.67	10.14
1980-1990	0.05	0.02	0.07	6.22	6.15
1990-1995	0.09	1.24	1.33	2.50	1.17

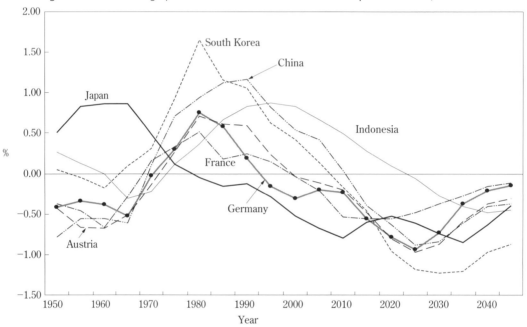

Figure 1-11. First Demographic Dividend in Selected Asian and European Countries, 1950-2050

Source: Mason, A. (2005) *Demographic Transition and Demographic Dividends in Developed and Developing Countries*, Paper Presented at the United Nations Expert Group Meeting on Social and Economic Implications of Changing Population Age Structure, Mexico City, August 31-September 2.

the first demographic dividend for each country. The calculated results for five Asian and three European countries are presented in Figure 1-11. It can be easily noted that the length of the first demographic dividend is considerably longer among the Asian countries than in the European countries. For instance, in the case of Germany, it lasts only 15 years from 1975 to 1990. Similarly, it is 15 years for Italy, and 25 years for France. In contrast, the length of the first demographic dividend is 40 years for China and the Republic of Korea. In addition, the magnitude of the first demographic dividend is also considerably larger in Asian countries than in European countries. It is particularly large in such countries as China and the Republic of Korea where the fertility level plummeted at unprecedented rates.

It is worth remarking that the application of the 2000 U.S. age profiles of consumption and labor income to Japanese data has produced a considerably different result. That is, the length of the first demographic dividend for Japan lasts only for 28 years (1950-1978) rather than for 46 years (1949-1995).

Figure 1-12. Second Demographic Dividend in Selected Asian and European Countries, 1950-1995

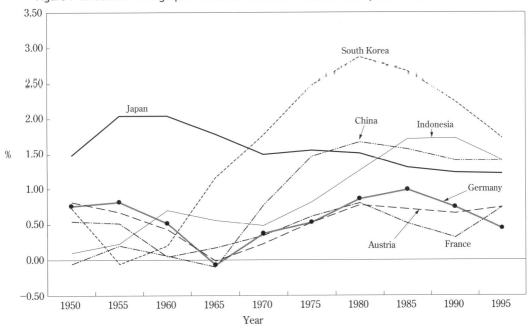

Source: Mason, A. (2005) *Demographic Transition and Demographic Dividends in Developed and Developing Countries*, Paper Presented at the United Nations Expert Group Meeting on Social and Economic Implications of Changing Population Age Structure, Mexico City, August 31-September 2.

This result suggests that the choice of the age profiles of consumption and production makes substantial differences in terms of the magnitude and timing of the first demographic dividend.

Figure 1-12 compares the timing and length of the second demographic dividend for three Asian countries and three European countries. The plotted results clearly indicate that all three Asian countries enjoy a considerably larger second demographic dividend compared to the three European countries. It is also worth noting that unlike the case of the first demographic dividend, the computed result for the second demographic dividend for Japan, based on the 2000 U.S. age profiles of consumption and labor income, is, by and large, comparable to that presented in Figure 1-7.

5 Lifecycle Deficits and Lifecycle Reallocations

NTA, which measures intergenerational flows for a certain period of time (usually a calendar or fiscal year), is governed by the following relationship (Mason et al., 2009):

$$y^l + r(K + M) + \tau_g^+ + \tau_f^+ = C + I_K + I_M + \tau_g^- + \tau_f^- \tag{1}$$

where y^l = labor income; rK = returns to capital; rM = returns to land and credit; τ_g^+ = transfer inflows from the public sector; τ_f^+ = transfer inflows from the private sector; C = consumption; I_K = investment in capital; I_M = investment in credit and land; τ_g^- = transfer outflows to the government; τ_f^- = transfer outflows to the private sector.

In addition, the lifecycle deficit, which is the difference between consumption and production, is matched by age reallocations consisting of reallocations through assets and net transfers as expressed below:

$$\underbrace{C - y^l}_{\text{Lifecycle deficit}} = \underbrace{\underbrace{y^A - S}_{\text{Asset reallocations}} + \underbrace{\tau_g^+ - \tau_g^-}_{\text{Net public transfers}} + \underbrace{\tau_f^+ - \tau_f^-}_{\text{Net private transfers}}}_{\text{Age reallocations}}_{\text{Net transfers}} \tag{2}$$

Transfers are further broken into net public transfers and net private transfers consisting of bequests and *inter vivos* transfers. *Inter vivos* transfers include transfers within the households (intra-household transfers) and between the households (inter household transfers). The estimated values for the totals are adjusted on the basis of the NIPA values, thus insuring consistency with NIPA. Labor income, however, does not exactly adjusted to NIPA counterpart, because the income of unincorporated firms includes returns to labor and capital. Based upon a simplifying assumption, we allocate two-thirds of this income to labor and one-third to capital.

A fuller explanation of NTA's basic concept, the crucial computational assumptions utilized, and the definitions of key variables are NTA home page (http://www.ntaaccounts.org). We will confine ourselves to discussing the estimated results for a few Asian countries (primarily Japan for the sake of convenience, in addition to Taiwan, Thailand, and Indonesia) and the United States. For discussion purposes, 'familial transfers' and 'private transfers' refer to the same sources, transfers coming from other family members of the same or different households, and '*inter vivos* transfers' is used in the text referring to familial or private transfers without bequests.

Figure 1-13 presents the changing pattern of three components of reallocation of the lifecycle deficits for Japan from 1989 to 2004. The three components include reallocations through assets, public transfers, and private transfers. Panel A illustrates the population-weighted reallocation of the lifecycle deficits observed in 1989, Panel B that observed in 1994, Panel C that observed in 1999, and Panel D that observed in 2004.

The share of public resources going into the young population diminished over the fifteen-year period. The young age group, 0 to 19 years old, receives transfers from the government nearly as much as transfers from the family. While, public health transfers to the young generation are almost negligible (Ogawa et al., 2007), public transfers to the young generation in terms of education is significant starting from approximately 5 years of age. Public transfers in education reach a peak for primary to senior school aged children. The tendency of public transfers to decline over time may be induced by the decreasing population of school-aged children. More importantly, *inter vivos* transfers are still significant towards these non-productive age groups since they commonly coreside with their parents, which facilitate *inter vivos* transfers.

Productive age groups pay tax and social security contributions to the government, which are reallocated through public transfers. Thus, those who belong to approximately 20 to 60 age groups

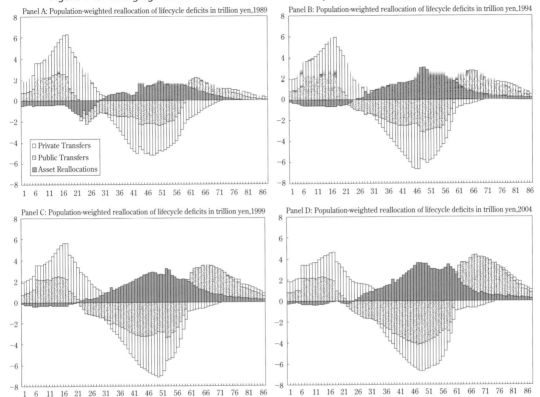

Figure 1-13. Changing Pattern of Reallocation of the Lifecycle Deficits for Japan, 1989 to 2004

Source: Nihon University Population Research Institute Projection based on *Family Income and Expenditure Survey* (1999) Statistics Bureau, Ministry of Internal Affairs and Communications, Japan.

experience negative net benefits of public transfers. The peak age of tax burden tends to move forward over time that reflects population aging as displayed in Figure 1-13. Asset reallocations, on the other hand, show an unclear pattern. Positive asset reallocation means that people receive returns through investing their assets, while negative asset reallocation means an investment. Negative asset reallocation occurs at young ages, mainly in the form of an investment in public facilities. Positive assets reallocations reach a peak in a person's late 40s or early 50s, comprising mostly of the returns of private investment, the majority of which is property income. Large asset reallocations in the early 20s to 50s age groups in 1999 compared to those of 1989 indicates that asset investments are becoming important to finance deficits. Perhaps not as much as public transfers, but the returns from their investment are definitely significant in financing deficits beyond 50s.

Lifecycle deficits change from negative to positive for the elderly, approximately starting at early 60s, which mean that consumption is relatively greater than production (Figure 1-13). Public transfers, small familial transfers, and significant asset reallocation particularly in recent years, are ways of compensating for the positive deficits which occur in their 60s.

Figure 1-14 shows details of the changing pattern of the components of reallocation to finance consumption of the young elderly (65-84) and the old elderly (85+) from 1989 to 2004. Due to the

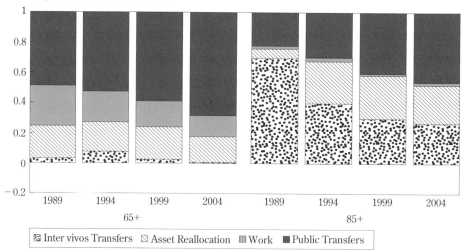

Figure 1-14. Finance of Consumption, Old Dependents (Age 65+) and Older Dependents (85+), Japan, 1989, 1994, 1999, 2004

underlying assumptions, changes in reallocation components of lifecycle deficits imply changes in labor participation, living arrangement, and social security program or public pension benefits paid to the elderly. Labor income profiles and disposable income profiles draw on the outflow of both public and private transfers. While labor income can be estimated based on individual profiles, some components of disposable income have to be assigned only to the household head, such as cash transfers received from or given to other households. Thus, the results on reallocation through public transfers reflect the profiles of labor participation. On the other hand, the underlying assumption to estimate intra household transfers or *inter vivos* transfers may reflect the living arrangement pattern, such as three-generational households.

Table 1-1 shows that around 22% of the elderly are working to finance their consumption in 1996, and the reallocation of lifecycle deficits displayed in Figure 1-14 indicate that approximately 25% and 21% of the elderly of 65 and over consumption is financed through their labor income in 1989 and 1994 respectively. Some of the elderly continue working to finance their deficits. However, even though the retirement age is rising beyond 60 years old, the role of labor income has declined over time. Around 15% of the elderly finance their consumption by labor income in 2004. This implies that the contribution of labor income declined by 10% points within 15 years. As will be indicated later, the contribution of labor income is now substituted by public pension. Labor income profiles, which include both earnings and self-employment income, are in a steep downward decline at approximately 65 years old with the earning components typically diminish by 70s as shown in Figure 1-6. Labor income finances approximately 20% of the consumption of young elderly (65-84). Whereas the people working in the formal sector retire around 65, the self-employed continue to be productive until their late 90s with declining rates. As shown in Figure 1-14, labor income finances only about 2% of the consumption of the older aged. While the contribution of labor income to finance the consumption of the young elderly (65-84) has declined over time, the pattern of contribution of labor income to consumption of the 85 and over has been relatively stable over the 15 years from 1989 to 2004.

The maturity of public pension benefits has caused a substantial increase in the share of public resources allocated to the elderly, that is, for both the young elderly and the very old elderly. Public transfers cover around 10% to 76% of consumption of the young elderly from 1989 to 2004 and approximately 28% to 58% of the consumption of the older elderly during the same period. Thus, the role played by public transfers is more critical for the young elderly than for the older elderly. Old-age pension and medical care services are the main public programs enjoyed by the elderly as benefits of universal coverage. The role of public transfers is becoming increasingly important as more elderly retire and receive pension benefits.

Public transfers play an increasingly role in financing the elderly consumption crowding out the role of *inter vivos* transfers. As a result, transfers from family only marginally finance the consumption of the 65 to 84 elderly as shown in Figure 1-14 and remains at low level. This partially could be explained by the decreasing in three-generational families from 66% in 1985 to 51% in 2000. *Inter vivos* transfers to the 65 and older elderly were already low in 1989, but declined even further between 1994 and 2004, contributing approximately 8%, 2%, and -0.2% towards the consumption of the elderly in 1994, 1998, and 2004 respectively. Judging from the recent trends of aging population, *inter vivos* transfers will most likely continue to decline in the future. Today, fewer and fewer children feel obliged to support their parents materially. However, time transfers may not decline as much as in-kind or cash transfers, particularly those flowing from young women towards their parents in the case of Japan. Since there is a trend to emphasize the role of the family in taking care of the elderly in the government's recent programs, younger generations, particularly women, are expected to take care of their frail parents at home. Thus, it is quite possible that the value of time transfers will exceed the value of cash or in-kind transfers toward parents.

In contrast with the case of young elderly, greater *inter vivos* transfers flow from prime age groups flow towards the 85 and older elderly. The flow of *inter vivos* transfers, though declining over time, is significant, covering approximately 39% and 21% of their consumption in 1989 and 2004 respectively. This means that *inter vivos* transfers have reduced almost by half over a span of 20 years, replaced in the main by public transfers.

As *inter vivos* transfers diminish over time, asset reallocations tend to be relatively more important than *inter vivos* transfers do in financing the consumption of the elderly. For those who are older than 65, however, asset reallocations are far below the level of public transfers, and is also less in amount compared to the labor income the young elderly can earn. Working generations accumulate wealth by buying stocks, bonds, or other kinds of capital investment, expecting to receive the returns during their retirement as an alternative way to finance their consumption. Asset reallocations finance approximately 21% of consumption of the young elderly in 1989, significantly higher than 3% of familial transfers to the same age group in the same year. Unlike the pronounced decline in the contribution of labor income in financing lifecycle deficits, asset reallocations showed a less clear pattern.

Figure 1-14 shows that the reallocation through assets accumulations among the 65 and older age group is inferior compared to the labor income and the increasing amount of public pension benefits received. The elderly of 65 and older live independently by drawing upon increased public transfers, which crowd out private transfers and their retirement induced from the labor market. The public transfers also possibly crowd-out assets accumulations of the old cohort to secure their retirement. The role of asset reallocations in financing consumption of the very old elderly has declined from 1989 to 2004. Even though the proportion of asset reallocation was only around 19% in 2004, it increased from only 11% in 1999 and the role of asset reallocations in financing consumption of the retirees seem unobvious in the future.

It is interesting to compare Japan's 1999 results with those observed for the U.S. in 2000, Taiwan in 1998, Thailand in 1998, and Indonesia in 1996. Whereas the components of reallocation for the U.S. and Taiwan in Figure 1-15 include bequest, the results for Japan, Thailand and Indonesia do not.

Reallocations for financing the consumptions of the elderly in U.S and Japan are characterized in two ways; public transfers dominate the reallocation and low labor participation among the elderly as compared one with Indonesia and Thailand as depicted in Figure 1-15. Public transfers towards the elderly are also small in these developing countries. High public transfers in the U.S, Japan and Taiwan provide a strong incentive for the elderly to retire such that the labor incomes of the elderly of these countries finance only around 15% of their consumption. However, such incentives probably do not exist in developing countries with limited public transfers, particularly without a public pension scheme. Because the elderly in developing countries cannot rely on public transfers, alternative ways to finance their consumption are needed, e.g. working beyond their normal retirement age, particularly in the field of self-employment such as agriculture. Indonesia is one of the countries where the majority of the population relies on income from agriculture sectors. The elderly in the agricultural sector work beyond

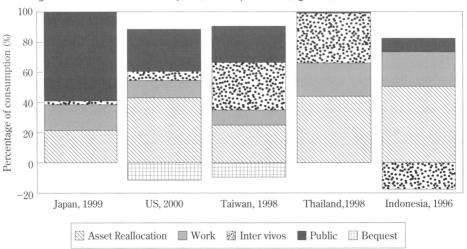

Figure 1-15. Finance of Consumption, Old Dependents (Age 65+) of Selected Countries

Source: Mason, A., Lee, R., Tung, A. -C., Lai, M. -S., Miller, T. (2009) "Population Aging and Intergenerational Transfers: Introducing Age into National Accounts" in *Developments in the Economics of Aging*, NBER and University of Chicago Press, pp.89-122.

the normal retirement age of formal sectors, financing approximately 39% of their consumption with their labor income. In Thailand where levels of labor in the field of agriculture are falling, labor income in financing the retirement of the elderly is less important, making up approximately 21% of their consumption. Yet, in developed countries, the role of labor income is even lower.

Public transfers to the elderly, consisting mainly of pension benefits and medical expenses, are important in the developed countries (Figure 1-15), like the U.S. and Japan. Japan surpasses the U.S. and Taiwan in public transfers to the elderly. While in 1999, approximately 59% of lifecycle deficits of the elderly aged 65 and over were financed through public transfers in Japan, only 37% and 29% of the consumptions of the same age group were financed in this way in the U.S. and Taiwan, respectively. Public transfers to the elderly in Japan are mostly in the forms of pension benefits and health expenditure, both being almost equal in importance (Ogawa et al., 2007). The role of pension benefits in financing consumption of the elderly becomes more significant as the pension scheme matures. The medical expenditure, on the other hand, increase gradually at steady rates. However, medical expenditure in the U.S, in contrast to that of Japan, has risen tremendously in addition to increasing pension benefits (Mason et al., 2009).

As there is an absence of a comprehensive social security system, public transfers to the retirees are almost non-existent. Taiwan was in a transition to a comprehensive social security system and as part of this process, introduced the National Health Insurance (NHI) in 1995 (Mason et al., 2009). By 1998, public transfers to the elderly of 65 and older in Taiwan were considerably less than those in the U.S. and Japan. The elderly in Taiwan spend relatively less on health compared to their counterpart in the U.S. (Lee and Mason, 2006). Moreover, the Taiwanese elderly finance their health expenditure through the NHI with a limited coverage than the young generations do (Mason et al., 2009). Comparing to other Asian countries such as Thailand or even Indonesia, however, public transfers in Taiwan are relatively higher. Thailand is still developing their social security programs and its coverage is still limited so that the public transfers to the elderly in Thailand appear to be relatively non-important.

In Thailand and Indonesia, where the public pension system has not fully developed yet, asset reallocations are an important source for the elderly to support their retirement. Around 44% and 79% of the elderly consumption are financed by asset reallocation in Thailand and Indonesia respectively (Figure 1-15). In these two countries, the income from assets is mainly from saving withdrawals, housing rentals, and sales on valuable durable goods. Smaller sources of income come from investment in stocks or returns on dividends. Both countries have been attempting to realize universal pension coverage, but the system has not fully developed and its coverage is still very limited.

Asset accumulations also play an important role for the elderly in the U.S. Unlike in developing countries, the income from assets in the developed countries is mainly constituted by investment in stocks and other financial assets. Asset reallocations significantly contribute to financing their high consumption, particularly high health consumption during the retirement period. Even though the savings rates declined over the last three to four decades in the U.S. (Mason et al., 2009), approximately 55% of the consumptions of the elderly are financed through asset reallocations. Since public transfers to the Japanese elderly are high, such as the generous social security system, asset reallocations are not as large as in the U.S. As stated, Taiwan is in transition, and the elderly rely on public transfers and other means of reallocation for their retirement. Since only limited public transfers are available to the Taiwanese elderly, asset reallocations and familial transfers are still considerably large.

As discussed in the earlier section, the level and nature of family support vary substantially with the level of economic development. In most developing countries of Asia, families provide significant financial and non-financial support to the elderly. In the developed countries, however, public transfers play a greater role in supporting the elderly, although families still provide their elderly dependents with other types of support. As is the case of Japan, the elderly in the U.S. rely only to a small extent on the private transfers, which cover around 7.2% of their total consumption. In contrast, the role of private transfers in Taiwan and Thailand are considerably higher.

6　Concluding Remarks

This paper has examined some of the important socioeconomic impacts of population aging in Asia and Europe, by drawing upon the computed results of the NTA project, ranging from the first and second demographic dividends to the lifecycle reallocations. We have also analyzed the pattern of living arrangements for the elderly in Asia and Europe, and the changing pattern of public support programs (medical and old-age pension programs) in relation to a given country's overall economic development.

Generally, judging from numerous past experiences of many industrialized countries in the West, demographic solutions have not been successful to cope with the various issues arising from population aging. For instance, low fertility is resistant to policy, and immigration measures are of limited help. Yet the utilization of the first demographic dividend as well as the accumulated second demographic dividend among the elderly seem to have some promising potential in placing a country's economic growth on a steady growth path. In addition, some of the NTA results derived from the lifecycle deficits provide a solid base for formulating effective long-term policies to cope with the adverse effects of population aging.

References

Bongaarts, J., Zimmer, Z. (2001) "Living Arrangements of Older Adults in the Developing World: An Analysis of DHS Household Surveys" *Policy Research Division Working Paper* 148, New York: Population Council.

Goode, W. J. (1963) *World Revolution and Family Patterns,* London: Free Press of Glencoe.

Jones, G. W. (1988) *Consequences of Rapid Fertility Decline for Old Age Security*, Paper Presented at the IUSSP Seminar on Fertility Transition in Asia: Diversity and Change, Bangkok: Chulalongkorn University, 28-31 March.

Kamnuansilpa, P., Wongthanavasu, S. (2002) "Health and Health Policy in Thailand" *NUPRI Research Paper Series* 74, Tokyo: Nihon University Population Research Institute.

Lee, R., Mason, A. (2006) "Back to Basics: What is the Demographic Dividend" *Finance & Development* 43, pp.16-17.

Lesthaeghe, R., Willems, P. (1999) "Is Low Fertility Only A Temporary Phenomenon in the European Union?"

Population and Development Review 25, pp.211-228.

Management and Coordination Agency (1997) *Brief Summary of the Fourth International Comparative Survey of the Elderly*, Tokyo: Gyosei Printing Co.

Martin, L. G. (1988) "The Aging of Asia" *Journal of Gerontology* 43(4), pp.S99-S113.

Mason, A. (ed.) (2001) *Population Change and Economic Development in East Asia: Challenges Met, and Opportunities Seized*, Stanford: Stanford University Press.

Mason, A. (2005) *Demographic Transition and Demographic Dividends in Developed and Developing Countries*, Paper Presented at the United Nations Expert Group Meeting on Social and Economic Implications of Changing Population Age Structure, Mexico City, August 31-September 2.

Mason, A., Lee, R. (2006) "Reform and Support Systems for the Elderly in Developing Countries: Capturing the Second Demographic Dividend" *Genus* LXII(2), pp.11-35.

Mason, A., Lee, R., Tung, A.-C., Lai, M.-S., Miller, T. (2009) "Population Aging and Intergenerational Transfers: Introducing Age into National Accounts" in *Developments in the Economics of Aging*, NBER and University of Chicago Press, pp.89-122.

McDonald, P. (2005) *Low Fertility in Singapore: Causes, Consequences and Policies*, Paper Presented at the Forum on Population and Development in East Asia, Beijing, May 16-17.

Myers, G. C. (1988) *Demographic Ageing and Family Support for Older Persons*, Paper Presented at the Expert Group Meeting on the Role of the Family in Care of the Elderly, Mexico City.

Ogawa, N. (1988) "Population Change and Welfare of the Aged" *Asian Population Studies Series* (*Frameworks for Population and Development Integration*) 92, United Nations ESCAP, Bangkok, Thailand, pp.105-132.

Ogawa, N. (1992) "Economic Factors Affecting the Health of the Elderly" in Kane, R. L., Evans, J. G., Macfadyen, D. (eds.). *Improving Health in Older People: A World View*, Oxford: Oxford University Press, pp.627-646.

Ogawa, N. (2005) "Population Aging and Policy Options for A Sustainable Future: The Case of Japan" *Genus* 61, pp.369-410.

Ogawa, N., Kondo, M., Tamura, M., Matsukura, R., Saito, T., Mason, A., Tuljapurkar, S., Li, N. (2003) *Long-term Perspectives for Japan: An Analysis Based on A Macroeconomic-Demographic-Social Security Model with Emphasis on Human Capital*, Tokyo: Nihon University Population Research Institute.

Ogawa, N., Lee, S.-H., Matsukura, R. (2005) "Health and its Impact on Work and Dependency Among the Elderly in Japan" *Asian Population Studies* 1(1), pp.121-145.

Ogawa, N., Mason, A., Matsukura, R., Nemoto, K. (2007) "Population Aging and Health Care Spending in Japan: Public- and Private-sector Responses" in Clark, R., Ogawa, N., Mason, A., *Population Aging, Intergenerational Transfers and the Macroeconomy*, Cheltenham, UK, and Northampton, MA: Edward Elgar, pp.192-223.

Ogawa, N., Matsukura, R. (2005) *The Role of Older Persons' Changing Health and Wealth in An Aging Society: The Case of Japan*, Paper Presented at the United Nations Expert Group Meeting on Social and Economic Implications of Changing Population Age Structure, Mexico City, August 31-September 2.

Ogawa, N., Retherford, R. D. (1993a) "The Resumption of Fertility Decline in Japan: 1973-92" *Population and Development Review* 19(4), pp.703-741.

Ogawa, N., Retherford, R. D. (1993b) "Care of the Elderly in Japan: Changing Norms and Expectations" *Journal of Marriage and the Family* 55(3), pp.585-597.

Ogawa, N., Retherford, R. D. (1997) "Shifting Costs of Caring for the Elderly Back to Families in Japan" *Population Development Reviews* 23(1), pp.59-94.

Phananiramai, M., McCleary, W. (1998) *A Study on the Extension of Social Security to the Self-employed*, Research Paper Prepared for the Social Security Office, Bangkok: Thailand Development Research Institute.

Population Problems Research Council (2004) *National Survey on Population, Families and Generations*, Tokyo: Mainichi Newspapers.

Retherford, R. D., Ogawa, N., Sakamoto, S. (1999) "Values and Fertility Change in Japan" in Leete, R. (ed.). *Dynamics of alues in Fertility Change*, Oxford: Oxford University Press, pp.121-147.

Sinding, S. W. (2002) "Policies at the End of the Demographic Transition: A Speculation" *East Asian Perspectives* 13, pp.85-97.

Treas, J., Logue, B. (1986) "Economic Development and the Older Population" *Population and Development Review* 12(4), pp.645-673.

United Nations (1987) "Global Trends and Prospects of the Age Structure of Population: Different Paths to Ageing" in *Papers and Proceedings of the United Nations International Symposium on Population Structure and Development*, New York: United Nations.

United Nations (2002) *World Population Ageing 1950-2050*, New York: United Nations.

Chapter 2

The Current Status of the Earned Income Tax Credit in Korea and the Implication to Japan: Earned Income Tax Credit or Reduced Tax Rate?

Myoung-Jung Kim

1 Introduction[1]

On January 1, 2008, South Korean government introduced an Earned Income Tax Credit (EITC) to boost work incentives of the working poor through supporting income of the tax system and achieving fairness and efficiency of the social system management by establishing new infrastructure. Simply put, the EITC is a subsidy to support the work for low earners. This is not familiar to the people in Japan, but the system is known to economists. In 1975, the system was introduced to the United States, and currently the system has been adopted in many countries, such as the United Kingdom, Canada, France, Sweden, Netherland, South Korea, and so on; it has passed more than a quarter of a century since the introduction to the United States.

As Japan does not have a similar system, it might be difficult to fully understand the EITC. To explain more specifically, it is an income support for the work system done by supporting one's real income. Kamakura (2010) explains the EITC as follows. "The EITC is, literally, an integrated system of social security benefits and tax credit. To be specific, income taxpayers are offered tax credit, and those who cannot be exempted or are below the minimum taxable ceiling are provided cash benefits. Source of the idea originates from Freedman's negative income tax."[2]

It aims to increase work incentives of the working poor who earn low income or suffer from economic difficulties by providing financial incentives which are calculated on the basis of their earned income. 'Welfare' is the conventional policy of public assistance, which supports income up to a certain level and is not related to whether the person is working or not; on the other hand, the EITC pursues 'Workfare', that provides assistance in order to increase total income as the working poor work. Therefore, the system can achieve anti-poverty and ease income disparity, and it aims to induce the participation to labor market from the dependence on welfare benefit, by providing financial assistance to the working poor.

2 Background and Process of the Introduction of the EITC in South Korea

In this section, it is discussed that the poverty rate and the current situation of the working poor in

---

1 This paper supplemented and revised Kim, M. -J. (2011) *The Current Situation of the Korean Earned Income Tax Credit (EITC)* NLI Research Institute, 2011/10/24 with latest contents and information.
2 Retrieved from Kamakura, H. (2010) "Overview of the EITC in Foreign Countries" *Survey and Information-ISSUE BREIF* 678.

South Korea by utilizing OECD data and precedent studies to explain the background of the implementation of the EITC.

Figure 2-1 illustrates relative poverty rates among OECD countries and relative poverty rates[3] among the working households. Relative poverty rate of South Korea in the mid-2000s (14.6%) highly outweighs the OECD average (10.6%).

To understand the current situation of the working poor in South Korea, Lee et al. (2010) classifies household in two groups, 'elderly household' and 'non-elderly household' based on OECD data, and compares South Korean data with the OECD average. As a result, 'poverty rate of elderly household' is 48.5% and it exceeds the average OECD of 13.7%. The high poverty rate of elderly household in South Korea is attributed to immature public pension system in terms of payments. Meanwhile, poverty rate of the non-elderly household is 10.9%, and there is a relatively small difference with the OECD average of 10.1%. However, 'elderly household' accounts for 21.9% of all poor households and the figure is smaller than 32.1% of OECD; labor problem of working households in South Korea seems to be bigger (Table 2-1).

The high economically active household ratio that consists of the all poor households in South Korea is attributable to relatively low population aging rate, low rate of participation to labor market of young generation based on employment mismatch, high ratio of non-regular workers with relatively low income level among employees, South Korean government's insufficient countermeasures for social security for economically active households, and so on.

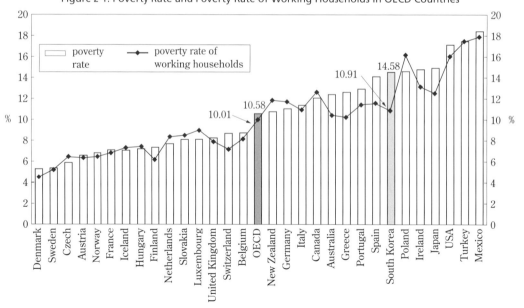

Source: OECD (2009) *Employment outlook,* Geneva: OECD.

---

[3] According to definition of OECD, the ratio of the people's equivalent disposable income (disposable income of households divided by square root of the number of households) does not reach half of the entire nation people's median value.

Table 2-1. Comparison in Rate of the Working Poor (South Korea and the OECD Average)

(Unit: %)

		South Korea	OECD Average
	Poverty Rate of the Population	14.6	10.6
Age of the Householder	Poverty Rate of Elderly Households (Poor Elderly Households/Elderly Households)	48.5	13.7
	(A)Poverty Rate of Non-Elderly Households (Poor Non-elderly Households/Non-elderly Households)	10.9	10.0
	Ratio of Elderly Households among All Households (Poor Elderly Households/All Poor Households)	21.9	32.1

Note: Elderly Households: Age of the householder is 65 and above.
Non-Elderly Households: Age of the householder is 15-64.

Source: The author made the table based on Lee, B. -H. et al. (2010) *Working Poor and Policies for Support,* Korea Labor Institute, p.14, OECD (2009a) "Is Work the Best Antidote to Poverty?" *Employment Outlook,* Geneva: OECD, and OECD(2009b) "The Jobs Crisis: What Are the Implications for Employment and Social Policy" *Employment Outlook,* Geneva: OECD.

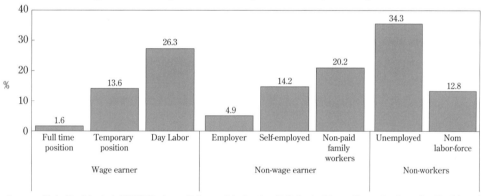

Figure 2-2. Poverty Rate of Working Generation by Working Status

Souece: Noh, D. -M. et al.(2009)*Study on Reform of Activation Policies in Korea,* Korea Institute for Health and Social Affairs.

The main reason of poverty among economically active households in South Korea is precarious work. Noh et al. (2009) estimates that about one-third of the unemployed and about a quarter of day laborers are in the poor class (Figure 2-2).

Kim (2009) presents that as the size of an enterprise gets smaller, the years of employment become shorter and the ratio of low income workers gets higher. To be specific, 18.8% of male and 39.1% of female workers in companies of 1-4 workers are low wage employees[4] while 0.7% of male and 4.0% of female workers receive low wage in companies with more than 1000 employees (Figure 2-3).

From the result, South Korean government introduced the EITC system to address the income gap and the increase of the working poor issues, which stems from globalization of economy in recent years, changes in industrial structure, and expansion of non-regular workers. Especially, 'the secondary poor[5]', which consist of the working poor, are put in difficult situations to escape from poverty as they easily

---
[4] The paper defines low-wage as the wage is lower than 50% of the median wage.
[5] An income group that earns income is less than 120% of the minimum cost of living and is excluded from receiving benefits of the National Basic Livelihood Security System, a public assistance system of Korea.

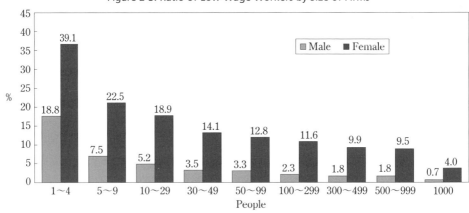

Figure 2-3. Ratio of Low-Wage Workers by Size of Firms

Note: The paper defines low-wage as the wage lower than 50% or 50% of them edian wage.
Souece: Kim, Y. -M. (2009) *The Increase of Smal Firms in Korea: Implications for Job Mobility,* and Noh, D. -M. et al. (2009) *Study on Reform of Activation Policies in Korea,* Korea Institute for Health and Social Affairs.

Table 2-2. Composition of the Social Security Network Before and After the Implementation of the EITC

	The General Public	The Working Poor (The Secondary Poor)	The Poor
Before the Introduction of EITC (Two Social Safety Nets)	Social Insurance (1st Safety Net)		National Basic Living Security System (2nd Safety Net)
After the Introduction of EITC (Three Social Safety Nets)	Social Insurance (1st Safety Net)	The EITC (2nd Safety Net)	National Basic Living Security System (3rd Safety Net)

Source: Korean National Tax Service website.

become excluded from receiving public assistance like the National Basic Living Security System[6] and public social insurance for health, unemployment and so on. By 2002, the secondary poor's coverage rate of social insurance was 36.7% for the national pension, 27.7% for the employment insurance, 59.7% for the occupational health and safety insurance and 98.2% for the health insurance. If the health insurance is excluded, a considerable number of the secondary poor are ruled out from the public social security net[7]. To address the problem, South Korean government aims to raise working incentives by linking work and payment of the social insurance. South Korea introduces the EITC for the first time in Asia to shape the environment that promotes the working poor's economic independence and anti-poverty, and to expand and reform the social security network.

That is, by implementing the EITC, South Korean social security network has changed from the two-level system which is composed of public social insurance and public assistance (the National Basic Living Security System) public to the three-level system, and income security system gets more cordial (Table 2-2).

---

6 It corresponds to Japanese Livelihood Assistance System.
7 Cho, S. -J. et al.(2008) *Earned Income Tax Credit and Female Labor Supply: Empirical Analysis and Policy Issues,* Korean Women's Development Institute, p.51.

3 Process and Overview of South Korean EITC

3.1 Process and Changes of the EITC

In 2003, the presidential transition committee of the former president Moo-Hyun Noh proposed the implementation of the EITC, and the proposal was legislated. The EITC system related laws and regulations (Clause 2 and Clause 13, Article 100 of the Tax Reduction and Exemption Control Act) were enacted on December 26, 2006, and it was implemented from January 1, 2008; benefits have been paid since September 2009[8] (Table 2-3).

After the introduction of the EITC, amendments have been announced and the coverage has been expanded gradually. For example, the standard of household has been changed in the amendment of the year 2011, and families without dependent children (married households) also received benefits. Due to the amendment of the 2012, the elderly households of over 60 without a spouse or a child whom they support have been eligible since 2013. In addition, due to the amendment of 2013, the amount of benefits has increased since 2015 and benefits for children have been established. Please refer to Table 2-4 for main contents.

Table 2-3. Process of Introduction and History of the EITC in South Korea

Period	Main Contents
Feb-03	The presidential transition committee of the former president, Moo-hyun Noh, proposed implementation of the EITC.
Aug-05	Government decided to implement the EITC.
Oct-05	'Team for Infrastructure to Comprehend Income' was established in the National Tax Service.
Dec-05	'Organization of Panning EITC' was established in Ministry of Finance and Economy.
Dec-06	EITC related laws and regulations (Tax Reduction and Exemption Control Act) were enacted.
Jan-08	EITC was implemented.
Dec-08	Tax Reduction and Exemption Control Act was revised → Scope of eligibility and maximum amounts of annual benefits were expanded.
Dec-08	- Scope of eligibility: Households of at least two dependent children → Households with children
Dec-08	- Annual maximum amounts of benefits: 800 thousand won → 1.2 million won
Sep-09	EITC payment began.
Sep-12	Tax Reduction and Exemption Control Act was revised → Scope of eligibility and maximum amounts of annual benefits were expanded.
Sep-12	- Scope of eligibility: Households with dependent children → Households without children
Sep-12	- Maximum amounts of benefits: 1.2 million won → 2 million won
Sep-12	- Criteria of house: Homeless or households of only one house of 50 million won and less in terms of market price → Homeless or households of only one house of 60 million won and less
Sep-15	Expansion of the EITC benefits, establishment of the CTC, expansion of eligibility scope to the self-employed
Sep-15	Total amount of family members' assets (house, land, building, savings, etc.) is less than 100 million → Total amount of family members' assets (house, land, building, savings, etc.) is less than 140 million

Source: The author made the table based on Korean National Tax Service website, etc.

---

8 The South Korean EITC structure is basically referred to the EITC of the US.

Table 2-4. Main Changes in the South Korean EITC

Classification		1st Plan for Implementation	Revision in 2008 (Effective in 2009)	Revision in 2011 (Effective in 2012)	Revision in 2012 (Effective in 2013)	Revision in 2013 (Effective in 2014)	Revision in 2013 (Effective in 2015)
Target	Recipient	The employed		The employed, insurance sellers, door-to-door salesmen			The employed, insurance sellers, door-to-door salesmen, The self-employed
	Non-recipient	People who received benefits of the National Basic Livelihood Security System in the previous year			People who received benefits of the National Basic Livelihood Security System in March of the application year		
Criteria of Household		Two and more than two children under 18	A child under 18	Household without child, a married couple	Person over 60 without a spouse or a dependent child can apply		
Criteria of Total Income		Less than 17 million won of total amount for a married couple		Without dependent child: 13 million won a dependent child: 17 million won two dependent children: 21 million won three dependent children: 25 million won	Single household: 13 million won One earner household: 21 million won Dual earner household: 25 million won		
Criteria of House		Homeless	Homeless or households of only one house of 50 million won and less in terms of market price	Homeless or households of only one house of 60 million won and less in terms of market price			
Criteria of Assets		Total amount of family members' assets (house, land, building, savings, etc.) is less than 100 million					Total amount of family members' assets (house, land, building, savings, etc.) is less than 140
Maximum Benefit		—	1.2 million	Without dependent child: 700 thousand won A dependent child: 1.4 million won Two dependent children: 1.7 million won Three dependent children: 2 million won	Single household: 700 thousand won One earner household: 1.7 million won Dual earner household: 2.1 million won		

Source: The author supplemented the contents by referring to Lee, D. -H., Kwon, G. -H., Moon, S. -H. (2015) "Studies on policy effects of the EITC" *The Korean Association for Policy Studies* 24(2).

3.2 Purpose of the EITC

The South Korean EITC system has purposes to raise work incentives and to support real income of workers and business owners (except for professionals, paid since 2015) who have difficulties in economic independence due to low income by providing the EITC. EITC payment is calculated on the basis of family members, annual gross income, and so on. Maximum payment for a year has been expanded from 1.2 million won of the beginning to 2.1 million won at present[9].

Table 2-5 describes the differences between National Basic Living Security System and the EITC. In October 2000, National Basic Living Security System, a public assistance system that corresponds to Japanese Livelihood Assistance System, was adopted to address problems under the previous public

---

9 In the initial phase, main target was 'the secondary poor'; their household income is less than 120% of the minimum cost of living and they are excluded from receiving benefits of National Basic Living Security System. Working households whose annual gross income is less than 17 million won for the previous year received benefits up to 1.2 million won per year.

Table 2-5. Comparative Studies on the National Basic Living Security System and the EITC

	National Basic Living Security System	EITC
Year of Execution	2000	2008
Purpose of System	To secure livelihood security and promote self-support of the poor's	To boost the working poor (secondary poor)'s motivation to work and support real income
Eligibility	both working and non-working households below minimum cost of living	working households of the secondary poor
Payment Method	cash and in kind	tax deduction with benefits
Contents of Payment	Based on the principle of subsidiarity, payment is held	Setting phase-in, flat and phase-out ranges Maximum payment amount: 2.1 million won
Requirements for Recipients	income requirement, supporter requirement	gross income requirements, spouse requirement, house requirement, assets requirement
Characteristics of System	income security system	income support system associated with work
Relevant Laws	**National Basic Living Security Act**	Tax Reduction and Exemption Control Act
Application Method	principle of application + nomination by the government	principle of application

Source: The author made the table based on National Assembly Research Service (2011) *Current Situation of EITC and Improvement Plan*, etc.

assistance system[10].

3.3 Application Process of the EITC and Standard of Application

Unit of the assessment for South Korean income tax is an individual, while the EITC evaluates whether a household is eligible or not. Recipients of the EITC were limited to employees, and the eligibility has been expanded to the individual proprietor since 2015; however, proprietors without business registration and professionals like lawyers, patent agents, certified public accountants, physicians, pharmacists and so on are excluded. In the initial phase, employees were the only beneficiary of the EITC as income-capture rate of individual proprietors is lower than the rate of employees.

There are two ways to apply for the EITC: submitting an application within a certain period and after the period. If people apply for the EITC between 1st of May and 1st of June every year, they can apply for the assistance within a certain period. On the other hand, if a person applies after the period, between 2nd of June and 1st of December, 10% reduced subsidies for the EITC and the Child Tax Credit (CTC) [11] are provided. People who are eligible to apply for the EITC can apply for it by telephones[12], mobile phones, mobile websites and the internet or visiting tax office[13].

---

10 Kim, M. -J. (2004) "Social Economy Changes in Korea and Trends of Public・Private Social Expenditure after IMF System-Feature: Korean Social Policies after IMF System-" *Foreign Social Security Study* 146.

11 Since fiscal year 2015, a new CTC to provide up to 500,000 won per child annually for applicants who have a child to support is introduced.

12 Households verified to receive the EITC or the CTC based on income of the previous year.

13 If a person is not informed to apply, he or she can apply only by internet or visiting tax office.

To apply for the EITC and the CTC, following four standards are needed to be fulfilled.

①Standard for Household

- EITC: As of December 31 every year, the applicant has a spouse or a child under 18 to support, or the applicant is older than 60.
- CTC: As of December 31 every year, the applicant has a spouse or a child under 18 to support.

A child to support needs to meet all of the requirements.

· A child whom a householder supports or an adopted child who lives with a householder. However, grandchild and siblings can be included in his or her dependents[14].

· As of December 31 of the previous year, a child is younger than 18; however, there is no age requirement to the severely disabled.

· Annual gross income is 1 million won and less.

②Standard for Gross Income

- EITC: To receive benefits, gross income of a married couple for the previous year is less than the base amount illustrated in Table 2-6.

Following are calculation methods for types of income.

· Business income＝ total revenues×adjustment rates for industries

· Working income＝ total salaries

· Other income＝ total revenues－necessary expenses

· Interest·dividend·pension is included in total revenues

- CTC: annual gross income of a married couple is less than 40 million won.

③Standard for Housing: Standards for the EITC and CTC are Equivalent.

As of June 1ˢᵗ of the previous year, all members of a household do not own a house, or in case of

Table 2-6. Base Amount of Gross Income for Households

Classification of Household	Single Household	One Earner Household	Dual Earner Household
Base Amount of Gross Income	13 million won	21 million won	25 million won

Note: Gross income＝business income ＋ working income ＋ other income ＋ interest rate·dividend·pension income.

---

14 Grandchildren and siblings without a parent, In case a person supports grandchildren and siblings without a parent (including a case with only a father or a mother), annual gross income of a parent is 1 million won and less, or a parent is severely disabled under the Act on the Acceleration of Employment of the Disabled and Occupation Rehabilitation or is classified level 3 or higher under laws of compensation for 'May 18 Democratic Uprising ', In case a person supports grandchildren with a parent, the parent is younger than 18 and the parent's annual gross income is 1 million won and less.

Table 2-7. Assets and Evaluation Methods

Assets	Scope of Asset	Evaluation Method
Lands and Buildings (including houses)	Land and building subject to property tax	Standard value for taxation
Cars	Excluding for cars business use and trucks	Standard value for taxation
Jeonse Deposits (including deposits for lease)	Jeonse deposits for stores and house (including deposits for lease)	Rental deposits in the contract
Financial Assets	Total amount of savings over 5 million won for a person	Balance of financial assets
Securities	Total amount of stocks and bonds, installment savings, installment, bank balance, saving insurance, investment trust over 5 million won for a person	Listed stocks: final price
		Other securities: face value
Golf Membership	Membership for using a members-only golf course	Standard market price that National Tax Service announces
Rights to Acquire Real Estates	Rights of tenant as a member of an association	Settlement amounts of estimated value for existing building
	exclusive purchase rights for apartments	Payments until basic date of possession
	Redeemable land bonds	Face value
	Redeemable housing debenture	Face value

Note1: In Jeonse system, instead of paying monthly rents, the renter pays a lump sum of deposits (Jeonse) when a contract is signed instead of paying monthly rents.
Note2: Standard market price is utilized to establish the standard of assessment (acquisition tax, registration tax, fixed asset tax, etc.) on the local tax law.
Source: Korean National Tax Service website.

having a house, the market price of the house is less than 60 million won (only 1 house).

④Standard of Assets: Standards for the EITC and CTC are Equivalent.

As of June 1ˢᵗ of the previous year, total value of assets (a house, land, a building, savings, etc.) that all members of a household possess is less than 140 million won. Table 2-7 illustrates the scope of assets and evaluation methods in detail.

Besides the four standards, an applicant needs to be a South Korean citizen (including a person married with a South Korean citizen) and is not supported by other households.

3.4 EITC Payment System and Current Situation for Payment

The most important feature of the EITC payment system is that benefit amounts are divided into three parts based on working income level: phase-in range, flat range and phase-out range. In the phase-in range, the EITC benefits increase at a fixed rate as working income increases. In the flat range, maximum amount of benefits are provided regardless of increase in working income, and the EITC benefits decrease at a fixed rate as working income increases in the phase-out range. For example, up to 6 million won of annual gross income is in the phase-in range for single households, and the EITC benefits of single households increase as they work in this range. If single households earn 6-9 million won for annual gross income, they receive a fixed amount, 700 thousand won; if they earn 9-13 million won, the ETIC benefits that they receive a decrease as their annual gross income increases (Figure 2-4). Calculation method of the EITC for each type of households is described in Table 2-8.

In 2015, the CTC was introduced; applicants with dependent children can receive the maximum of 500 thousand won per child for a year as subsidies.

The number of households that receive the EITC increased from 522 thousand in 2010 to 846 thousand in 2013. The amount of benefits increased from 402 billion won to 774.5 billion won for the same period (Table 2-9), and the EITC has gradually been becoming a established system.

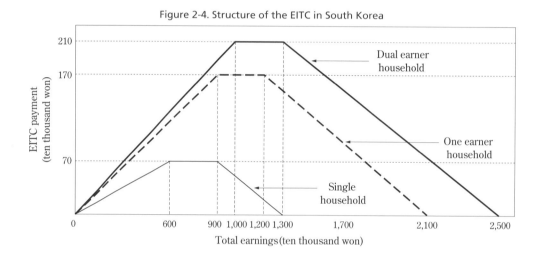

Figure 2-4. Structure of the EITC in South Korea

Table 2-8. Requirements to Receive the EITC and Calculation Methods for Households

Types of Households	Total Income	EITC Benefits
Single Household	Under 6 million won	Total income × (70/600)
	6 billion won ~ under 9 million won	0.7 million won
	9 million won ~ under 13 million won	0.7 million won − (total income − 9 million won) × (70/400)
One Earner Household	Under 9 million	Total income × (170/900)
	9 millio won ~ under 12 million won	1.7 million won
	12 million won ~ under 21 million won	1.7 million won − (total income − 12 million won) × (170/900)
Dual Earner Household	Under 10 million	Total income × (210/1000)
	10 million won ~ under 13 million won	2.1 million won
	13 million ~ under 25 million won	2.1 million − (total income − 13 million won) × (210/1200)

Note1: Single household: households over sixty without a spouse or children.
     One earner household: non-dual earner households with a spouse or children.
     Dual earner household: respective total income of the householder and the spouse is higher than 3 million in the previous year.
Note2: Total income= total salaries of earned income + (total revenue of business income × adjustment rate of industry).
Source: Korean National Tax Service website.

Table 2-9. Changes in the Amounts of the EITC Incentives and the Number of Recipient Households

(Unit: thousand households, billion won)

	Households that Applied for the EITC (A)	Recipient Households (B)	Payment Rate (B/A)	Ratio of B to the Whole Households	Amount of the EITC Incentives
2010	667	599	78.9	3	105
2011	930	752	80.9	4.3	614
2012	102	783	76.8	4.4	561.8
2013	106	846	79.8	4.6	774.5

Source: Korean National Tax Service website.

3.5   Extension of Coverage of the EITC and the CTC to the Self-Employed

From 2015, the scope of recipients of the EITC and the CTC has expanded from workers to the self-employed; however, professionals such as lawyers, patent agents, certified public accountants (CPA), physicians, pharmacists and so on but non-registered business operators are excluded. To receive the EITC or the CTC, the self-employed need to fulfill identical application criteria with those of the workers'. In addition, following procedures need to be completed beforehand.

· Registration of entrepreneur: by December 31st every year

· Final return on VAT: by January 26th every year

· Report on current status of business: business exempt from taxation need to report current status of business. By February 10th every year.

· Report on composite income tax: by June 1st every year

The self-employed, in common with the employed households, receive the EITC and the CTC benefits on the basis of 'total Income of a married couple'; however, considering that the self-employed have more difficulties in securing earnings than the employed do, the benefits to the self-employed is calculated by utilizing adjustment rates for industries. Table 2-10 demonstrates the adjustment rates for industries, and the rates are set differently for industries. That is, an industry with a high adjustment rate implies that its income support rate to the industry is low, so the adjustment rate is set high.

For example, if A manages a restaurant and earns annual gross revenue of 30 million won and his wife earns 10 million won in a year at a job, annual gross salary of A's household is 23.5 million won (Formula 1).

Formula 1) Annual gross income of A's household = (30 million won (A's annual gross revenue) × 0.45 (adjustment rate for a restaurant) + 10 million won (wife's total salary)) = 23.5 million

As this satisfies the criteria for base amount of gross income (dual income households) of Table 2-6, 1,916,250 won is provided as the EITC is based on the calculation of Formula 2.

Formula 2) 2.1 million won − ((23.5 million won ⟨gross income⟩ − 13 million won) × (210/1,200)) = 1,916,250 won

Table 2-10. Adjustment Rate for Industries

	Types of Industries	Adjustment Rate
A	Wholesale business	20%
B	Retailing, Car·components sales, real estate sales, agriculture·forestry·fishery, mining industry	30%
C	Restaurants, manufacture, construction, electricity·gas·steam·water business	45%
D	Accommodation business, transportation, finance·insurance, commodity brokerage, publication·image·media·information service, sewage·waste treatment·recycling·environmental restoration	60%
E	Service industry (real estates, professional science technology, business facility management, business support, education, health, social welfare, art, sports, leisure, repair, etc.)	75%
F	Leasing real estate, other leasing services, freelancer, individual housework service	90%

Source: Korean National Tax Service website.

Table 2-11. Ceiling of Annual Gross Revenue in Case of the Self-Employed Households Only with Business Income

(Unit: ten thousand won)

Business Classification	EITC			CTC
	Single Household	One Earner Household	Dual Earner Household	Household with Dependent Children
A	6,500	10,500	12,500	20,000
B	4,333	7,000	8,333	13,333
C	2,888	4,666	5,555	8,888
D	2,166	3,500	4,166	6,666
E	1,733	2,800	3,333	5,333
F	1,444	2,333	2,777	4,444

Source: Korean National Tax Service website.

However, in case of B who is engaged in leasing of real estate, even though B's annual revenue and his wife's salary is the same as the annual gross income of A's household, adjustment rate is higher and the amount of gross income increases; therefore, the amount of gross income does not satisfy the criteria for the base amount of gross income (dual income households) of Table 2-6, the EITC is not provided to B (Formula 3).

Formula 3) Annual gross income of B's household = 30 million won (B's annual gross revenue) × 0.9 (adjustment rate of leasing real estate) + 10 million won (wife's salary) = 37.5 million won

Table 2-11 represents the ceiling of annual gross revenue that self-employed households can apply for the EITC and the CTC; in order to be eligible for the benefits, business income needs to be the only income source for the self-employed.

4   Analysis on Effects and Challenges Ahead

Figure 2-5 explains the selection of leisure and labor hour as the EITC is introduced. As the EITC is implemented, indifference curve[15] of the people who are not participated in labor market shifts from U_0^I to U_1^I, and both the rates of participation in labor market and labor hours rise. In case of the people

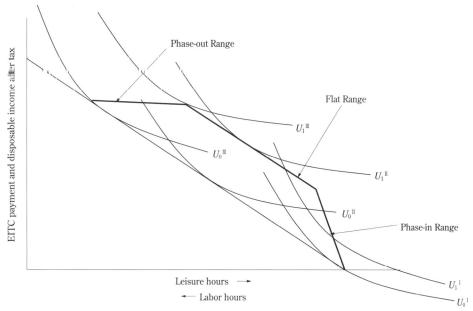

Figure 2-5. Selection of Leisure and Work Hour When the EITC is Introduced

Source: The author revised Hotz, V. J., Scholz, J. K. (2001) "The Earned Income Tax Credit" *National Bureau of Economic Research Working Paper* 8078.

who have already been participated, in a phase-in range (the range in which the work incentives increase at a fixed rate as the earned income rises), as the cost of choosing leisure instead of work increases, the increase of labor hours could be expected; however, both the substitution effect[16] and the income effect[17] occur, so its impact on work hour is not clear.

On the other hand, in a flat range (the range in which maximum amount of benefit is provided regardless of the increase and the decrease of earned income), as indifference curve shifts from U_0^{II} to U_1^{II} and the substitution effect does not exist, labor hours decrease. Finally, in a phase-out range (the range in which work incentives decrease as the earned income increases), indifference curve moves from U_0^{III} to U_1^{III} and labor hours decrease[18].

Precedent studies that analyzed effects of the EITC on labor supply can be largely classified into two groups: influences on participation in the labor market and influences on changes in labor hours. Due to the 8-year and relatively short history of the South Korean EITC, there are not many analysis on the effects. In this section, firstly, precedent studies on the EITC of the US that were implemented earlier than South Korea is introduced, and then results of recent studies on the South Korean EITC are presented.

---

15 Choosing either to work or not is based on utility level (level of satisfaction) of working and leisure. Indifference curve is a device to facilitate the comparison.
16 Effect that increase in wage rate makes labor supply more favorable, and labor supply increases.
17 Effect that increase in wage rate raises real wage, demand of leisure increases, and labor supply increases if leisure is a normal good (the demand for it increases as income increases).
18 Retrieved from Hotz, V. J., Scholz, J. K. (2001) "The Earned Income Tax Credit" *National Bureau of Economic Research Working Paper* 8078, and Lee, D. -W., Kwon, G. -H., Moon, S. -H. (2015) "Studies on policy effects of the EITC" *The Korean Association for Policy Studies* 24(2).

First, there are various studies on how the EITC of the US has influenced the participation in the labor market. Keane (1995) and Keane and Robert (1998) estimated that expansion of the EITC would increase labor force participation rate between 1984 and 1996. Dickert et al. (1995) also demonstrated the analysis result that participation in the labor market increases as income increases. Eliss and Liebman (1996) drew the conclusion that expansion of the EITC led to increase in single-mother families' labor participation rates.

Next, studies on influences of the EITC in labor hours are as follows. Contrary to the numerous studies that shows a positive correlation between the EITC and participation in the labor market, studies on the correlation between the EITC and labor hours do not necessarily converge.

Keane (1995), and Keane and Robert (1998) states that the EITC have positive effects on labor force participation as well as the labor market. On the other hand, Hoffmam and Seidman (1990), and Browsing (1995) conclude that expansion of the EITC reduces worker's labor hours.

What are the analysis results on introduction of the Korean EITC, which has shorter history than the EITC of the US? Using the NaSTab (National Survey of Tax and Benefit) Panel Data of Korea Institute of Public Finance, Song and Bahng (2014) analyzed the influences of the EITC on labor supply. The analyses are carried out for married couple households and single-parent households. The studies show the result that the rates of participation in labor market increases in the phase-in range (the range in which work incentives increases as earnings rise). On the other hand, married couple households reduce labor supply in both flat range (the range in which maximum amounts of incentives are provided regardless of increase and decrease in earnings) and phase-out range (the range in which work incentives decrease as earnings increases); single parent households show different results.

Utilizing 'Korean Welfare Panel', Lee et al. (2015) analyzed how the EITC benefits affect the labor market participation of low income class, labor hours and wages with Difference in Difference Analysis (DID Analysis)[19]. According to analysis results, employment rate of the group that receives the EITC (treatment group) increased from 70.51% before receiving (in 2008) to 78.20% (in 2012) after receiving, it increased by 7.69 percentage point. On the other hand, employment rate of the group that does not receive the EITC (control group) decreased from 71.85% in 2008 to 66.25% in 2012 by 5.62 percentage point decrease. In terms of labor hours, treatment group increased labor hours by 0.75 month while control group reduced labor hours by 0.19 month during the same period.

Chun (2010) classified households into 7 equal groups of the same number by their incomes and analyzed how the EITC influenced labor hours. As a result, the study found out that its effects on the increase in labor hours is not so significant.

Jeong and Kim (2015) analyzed the changes in criteria of the EITC payment in 2014, and the redistributive effects of the CTC on one-earner and dual-earner households, by using the household survey data of 2013. As a result, the EITC and the CTC have positive impacts on poverty rate and income redistribution; on the contrary, poverty rates of single-parent and elderly households increase among the one-earner households.

According to the results of studies in the South Korean EITC, some studies show that

Chapter 2 The Current Status of the Earned Income Tax Credit in Korea and the Implication to Japan: Earned Income Tax Credit or Reduced Tax Rate? **41**

implementation of the EITC increased the rate of participation in labor market or the labor hours while other studies present decrease in both the rate and the labor hours; results do not necessarily converge. However, there are many study results that the rates of participation in the labor market and labor hours have positive impacts on average. Especially, there are many studies that rated the participation in the labor market increases in phase in range (the range in which EITC benefits increase as earnings increase); therefore, to some extent, the South Korean EITC has achieved the goal set in the initial phase of the system.

However, there are many problems to be solved. First, securing financial resources needs to be prioritized. The scope of eligibility shows a tendency to expand. Budget for the EITC and the CTC was about 150 billion won in the initial period, and budget amounts increased to 1.7 trillion won in 2015. Although South Korean government plans to increase the range of eligible people (Table 2-12), the actual tax revenues are smaller than the budget due to recession, and securing financial resources is a difficult task for South Korean government.

In addition, self-employed households, exempt from professionals from 2015, can receive the EITC. As the self-employed have more difficulties in securing earnings than the employed do, the EITC reflects adjustment rates for industries of Table 2-10 and decides the recipients. However, adjustment rate for an industry is 90% and adjustment rates are high in general, so it is difficult for the self-employed to receive the EITC.

In order to provide more EITC benefits for the self-employed in financial difficulties, raising the income capture rate of the self-employed needs to be the first priority. As the income capture rate of the self-employed rises and the adjustment rates decrease, more self-employed households can benefit from the EITC.

South Korean government needs to focus on poor women that form the majority of the working poor for an implementation of the EITC. Many working women are engaged in insecure jobs such as

---

19 Estimating effect before and after implementing a policy, an equation like follows can be applied.

$Y_t = \beta_0 + \beta_1 d_t + \varepsilon_t$

In this equation, Y_t is a variable affected by execution of a policy. d_t is a dummy variable; it becomes 1 if affected by the policy, and it becomes 2 if unaffected. ε_t is an error term, and β_0 and β_1 are parameters for estimation. With estimation results based on this equation, it is possible to interpret that Y increased by policy implementation. However, it is difficult to judge that the policy is the only factor that increased Y. For instance, by enforcing an industrial policy in some prefectures, per capita GDP in the prefectures can increase, but it is impossible to say that the effect is solely due to the policy. That is, there is a possibility that the effect includes not only policy effect but also exogenous effects occur with time (time effect). DID Analysis divide into two groups: treatment group and control group. Treatment group is affected by policy while control group is not. That is, in order to examine net policy effect, it is necessary to analyze both those affected by policy (treatment group) and those unaffected by policy over time (control group).

	Treatment Group (Prefectures affected by Policy)	Control Group (Prefectures unaffected by Policy)
Before Implementing Policy	a	c
After Implementing Policy	b	d

As illustrated in the table above, policy effect before and after implementing on treatment group, prefectures affected by policy, (b−a) includes not only policy effect but also exogenous effect which occurs with time. On the other hand, policy effect before and after implementing on control group, prefectures unaffected by policy, (d−c) solely reflects exogenous effect over time. Therefore, by excluding (d−c) from (b−a), net policy effect that excludes exogenous effect with time is obtained. However, a point to notice is to assume exogenous effects on treatment group and control group is same. This is the main content of DID analysis.

Table 2-12. Plans to Expand the EITC in Phases

	Appling to Employees		Expanding to Proprietors	Fully Implementing
	1st Phase	2nd Phase	3rd Phase	4th Phase
	(2008~2010)	(2011~2013)	(from 2014)	(by 2030)
Eligible Households	Homeless households with two or more than two children	Household with one or more children	Household with one or more children	Household without any child is eligible
Number of Recipient Households	About 310 thousand households	About 90 thousand households	About 1.5 million households	About 3.6 million households
Annual Budget	About 150 billion won	About 400 billion won	About 1 trillion won	About 2 trillion 500 billion won

Source: Ministry of Strategy and Finance (2011) *Tax Law Revision in 2011(Plan)*.

part-time work, and they are susceptible to fall into poverty. In addition, once a person falls into poverty, it is difficult to escape from it. Those facts imply that South Korean government has scarcely implemented significant policies for working women to this day. Therefore, South Korean government needs to implement policies thoroughly for working women including the implementation of the ETIC from now on. The policies will promote female participation in the labor market, and it will lead to the establishment of safe environment for them to escape from poverty.

5   Implication to Japan

Currently, Japan explores possibilities for improvement in functions of the existing safety net. The South Korean EITC, which has been explained in this paper, is a meaningful case to review. In fact, scholars in Japan have paid interests to the EITC and discussed necessity of the system and adverse effects in case of introduction of the EITC. Morinobu (2008) suggests following four points as tasks in case of introduction of the EITC.

①To establish policy goals and clarify the target class to support

②To discuss and review the system and policies thoroughly and avoid incoherent policies

③To come up with measures against abuse of the system and the illegal receipt

④To establish structure for clear understanding of the income information as the tax office is in charge of operation and providing incentives

Applying these points to Japanese system, first, in terms of ①, setting working women and young households as the main target for the policy and establishing the same policy goals like South Korea has done are meaningful. Similar to South Korea, the number of the working poor among female workers and young households is increasing rapidly with the expansion of non-regularization of labor force in Japan. In addition, recently the South Korean government introduced 'Differentiated policies on the EITC based on the number of children.' As Japan has the same problem of declining number of children, it is a good policy to consider.

For ②, both countries need to implement policies that create the long and stable employment for as many people as possible rather than incoherent and money-pouring policies, and it is a shortcut to secure public finance. Waste of financial resources needs to be prevented under the context that pouring money is easier than creating stable employment.

For ③ and ④, Japan needs to utilize 'My Number System' which has been implemented since January 2016. However, even though South Korea introduced universal 'Resident Registration Number ID System' before Japan and is able to comprehend individuals' properties and savings, illegal receipt is happening in South Korea and grasping incomes of the self-employed still remains as an issue for government. Considering the South Korean cases, Japan needs to establish more effective system.

Some people state that the EITC needs to be implemented as an alternative plan for the reduced tax rate system. The Abe administration accepted the proposal of Komeito and decided to raise consumption tax rate to 10% in the near future and introduce a reduced tax rate system. However, there are a few dissenting voices from economists on the reduced tax rate system. Reasons for opposing the reduced tax rates are 'increase of political lobbying on the new reduced tax rate system,' 'misallocation of resources due to distortion in price system,' 'tax reduction is bigger for high-income earners with high consumption level, so the system is beneficial to high-income earners,' and 'failed cases in foreign countries.'

December 10 2015, Liberal Democratic Party and Komeito compromised to expand coverage to 'all perishable foods and processed foods', excluding alcohol and dining-out items. If the reduced tax rate is introduced and the new consumption tax increase to 10% from 8% is implemented, the government will lose about 1 trillion yen of its expected tax revenue. A part of the revenue shortfall will be covered by utilizing 400 billion yen earmarked for measures to help low-income earners, but no decision has been made on how to secure the remaining 600 billion yen. If financial resources for the remaining part are not secured, the government might consider reducing social security expenditures.

In fact, 1 billion yen, the cost of introducing the reduced tax rate, is comparable to 1.3 billion yen, the estimated cost of introducing the EITC by Shiroishi in 2010. Kawaguchi (2015) explains that there is no big difference between the costs of implementation of the reduced tax rate and the EITC based on the estimated result. He argues for feasibility of the EITC in Japan and necessity of active discussions for implementing the system.

The fundamental intent of the reduced tax rate is 'countermeasure for low-income earners'. However, there are other countermeasures for low-income earners. The EITC which was introduced in this paper is a good example. The EITC boosts the labor force participation rate in the labor market. Not weighted to the reduced tax rate system, Japanese government needs to review and consider the EITC which have shown certain results in the US and South Korea at the same time and implement more effective policies.

References

Browning, E. K. (1995) "Effects of the Earned Income Tax Credit on Income and Welfare" *National Tax Journal* 48(1), pp.23-43.

Cho, S. -J. et al. (2009) "Earned Income Tax Credit and Female Labor Supply" *Quarterly Journal of Labor Policy* 9(3).

Chun, Y. -J. (2010) "Employment and Welfare Effects of the EITC and the Minimum Wage System" *Monthly Labor Review* 2010 June.

Dickert, S., Houser, S., Scholz, J. K. (1995) "The Earned Income Tax Credit and Transfer Programs: A Study of Labor Market and Program Participation" in Poterba, J. M. (ed.). *Tax Policy and the Economy* 9, National Bureau of Economic Research and the MIT Press, pp.1-50.

Eissa, N., Hilary, W. H. (2004) "Taxes and the Labor Market Participation of Married Couples: The Earned Income Tax Credit" *Journal of Public Economics* 88, pp.1931-1958.

Hoffman, S. D., Seidman, L. S. (1990) *The Earned Income Tax Credit: Antipoverty Effectiveness and Labor Market Effects*, W. E. Upjohn Institute for Employment Research.

Hotz, V. J., Scholz, J. K. (2001) "The Earned Income Tax Credit" *National Bureau of Economic Research Working Paper* 8078.

Jeong, C. -M., Kim, J. -J. (2015) "The Redistributive Effects of Earned Income Tax Credit and of Child Tax Credit On One-Earner and Dual-Earner Household" *Korean Social Security Studies* 31(1), pp.233-253.

Kamakura, H. (2010) "Overview of the EITC in Foreign Countries" *Survey and Information-ISSUE BREIF* 678.

Kawaguchi, D. (2015) *Working toward the Introduction of Refundable Tax Credits*, RIETI Special Series: Priorities for the Japanese Economy in 2016.

Keane, M. P. (1995) "A New Idea for Welfare Reform" *Federal Reserve Bank of Minneapolis Quarterly Review* 19(2), pp.2-28.

Keane, M., Robert, M. (1998) "A Structural Model of Multiple Welfare Program Participation and Labor Supply" *International Economic Review* 39(3), pp.553-589.

Kim, G. (2008) "Study on Korean EITC" Refundable Tax Credits(EITC)" in Morinobu, S. (ed.). *Earned Income Tax Credit*, Chuokeizai-sha.

Kim, M. -J. (2004) "Social Economy Changes in Korea and Trends of Public·Private Social Expenditure after IMF System-Feature: Korean Social Policies after IMF System-" *Foreign Social Security Study* 146, pp.4-22.

Kim, M. -J. (2011) *The Current Situation of the Korean Earned Income Tax Credit (EITC)*, NLI Research Institute.

Kim, Y. -M. (2009) *The Increase of Small Firms in Korea: Implications for Job Mobility.*

Lee, B. -H., et al. (2010) *Working Poor and Policies for Support,* Korea Labor Institute.

Lee, D. -W., Kwon, G. -H., Moon, S. -H. (2015) "Studies on Policy Effects of the EITC" *The Korean Association for Policy Studies* 24(2), pp.27-56.

Ministry of Strategy and Finance (2011) *Tax Law Revision in 2011(Plan)*.

Morinobu, S. (2008) *Earned Income Tax Credit,* Chuokeizai-sha.

National Assembly Research Service (2011) *Current Situation of EITC and Improvement Plan.*

Noh, D. -M. et al. (2009) *Study on Reform of Activation Policies in Korea,* Korea Institute for Health and Social Affairs.

OECD (2009a) "Is Work the Best Antidote to Poverty?" *Employment Outlook,* Geneva: OECD, pp.165-210.

OECD (2009b) "The Jobs Crisis: What Are the Implications for Employment and Social Policy" *Employment Outlook,* Geneva: OECD, pp.17-115.

Song, H., Bahng, H. K. (2014) "The Effect of EITC on Job Creation in Korea" *The Korean Economic Review* 62(4), pp.129-167.

Tsuru, K. (2008) "Importance of EITC for Reforms on Tax·Social Security System" in Morinobu, S. (ed.). *Earned Income Tax Credit,* Chuokeizai-sha.

Chapter 3

Public Pension Schemes in China

Lan Liu

1 Introduction

In recent three decades, China has undergone the reform of the public pension system, especially the construction and transition of the financing system and the expansion of the financing resources. With the progress of China's public pension reform, the main pattern of social pooling and individual retirement account (SP & IRA) has been established and improved.

The current public pension system is mainly composed of two pillars: basic pension insurance for urban employees, and basic pension insurance for urban and rural residents. The financing resources of these two types above are different. Basic pension insurance for urban employees is financed on the basis of government, individual and employers, whereas the financing resources of basic pension insurance for urban and rural residents include individual contributions, collective subsidies and government subsidies.

At present, the population aging has become more serious than before. In 2010, the number of the older persons who were 60 years old and above was 177,648,705 accounting for 13.26%, and the number of older persons who were 65 years old and above was 118,831,709 accounting for 8.87% whereas accounting for 4.91% in 1982. Actually population aging has contributed to serious fiscal stresses in China and the public pension expenditures in China have increased sharply since the 1980s. Population aging, elderly dependency ratios and pension expenditures rising will definitely result in the great challenges to the public pension system. These are likely to get much worse over the next few decades in the absence of appropriate reforms. Therefore, it is necessary to reinforce the current positive outcomes of the pension reform since the 1990s and carry out the further improvement of the public pension system.

2 Background

2.1 Population Aging

With the rapid development of economy and society, the decline of fertility and mortality and the extension of population life expectancy, the population aging have taken on the trend of rapid growth. The data from the sixth population census in China showed that in 2010 the number of the older persons who were 60 years old and above was 177,648,705 accounting for 13.26%, and the number of older persons who were 65 years old and above was 118,831,709 accounting for 8.87% (Figure 3-1). In contrast with the data from the fifth population census in 2000, the percentage of the older persons aged 60 and above,

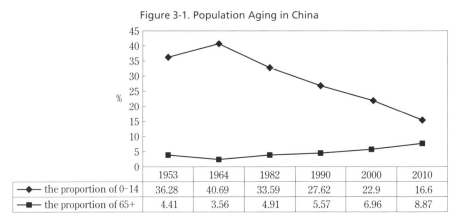

Figure 3-1. Population Aging in China

Source: The Population Census in China.

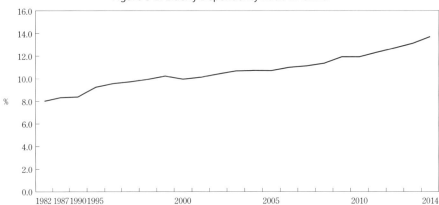

Figure 3-2. Elderly Dependency Ratio in China

Source: *China Statistical Yearbook 2015*, National Bureau of Statistics of China.

65 and above increased by 2.93%, and 1.91% respectively. The average number of each family household was 3.10 in 2010, with 0.34 person less than 3.44 persons of the fifth national census in 2000. By the end of 2015, the total number of older persons aged 60 and above was 222,000,000 accounting for 16.1%.[1]

According to "The Forecasting of Population Aging Trends for a Hundred Years" by China National Committee on Ageing (CNCA) older persons in China will reach 248 million in 2020, accounting for 17.17% of the total population; and the number of people who are 80 years old and above will reach 30.67 million accounting for 12.37% of the older persons. From 2005 to 2020, China's total population will undergo a net increase of 133 million, including the older persons in a net increase of 105 million with an average annual increase of more than 6.60 million people.

Population aging will bring about a range of demographic and socio-economic problems. One of the important issues is that the public pension expenditures in China have increased sharply since the 1980s, reflecting the rise in the elderly dependency ratios depicted in Figure 3-2.[2] In 1982, the elderly

---

1 See "Statistical Communique of the People's Republic of China on the 2015 National Economic and Social Development", National Bureau of Statistics of the People's Republic of China.

dependency ratio was 8.0%, then went up to 13.7% in 2014. Population aging, elderly dependency ratios and pension expenditures rising will definitely result in the great challenges to the public pension system. Therefore, the population aging has contributed to serious fiscal stresses in China which are more likely to get much worse over the next few decades in the absence of appropriate reforms.

2.2 Reform Progress of Public Pension System

The public pension system which is an important part of the social security system plays a very important and active role in the national economy and social development. Due to the special dual economic structure, the household registration system and other factors, in practice there must be regional and occupational differences for the public pension system, thereby in the process of pension system development the dual public pension system for urban and rural China has been built up.[3]

(1) Reform of Urban Public Pension System

After the state founding, the CPC Central Committee and State Council had attached great importance to the issues on social security of Chinese citizens. At the early years that the new China was founded, in February 1951, the State Council promulgated and implemented "Labor Insurance Regulations of the People's Republic of China" which marked the official launch of China's public pension insurance scheme. In 1956, the State Council decided to expand the implementation of the "Labor Insurance Regulations" to 13 industries and sectors such as commerce, foreign trade, etc.

In 1991, "Decisions of the Pension Insurance System Reform of the Enterprise Employees" issued by State Council stipulated: with economic development, gradually establishing a system composed of a basic pension insurance for urban employees,[4] enterprise supplementary pension insurance and individual saving pension insurance of employees. This "Decisions" changed the pattern that the public pension insurance was entirely financed by the state and the state enterprises to a new pattern which was supported by the state, the state enterprises and the individuals. The employees had to contribute to the public pension insurance. Taking into account the differences among enterprises and regions, the central government of each province, autonomous region and municipality might make specific provisions for the employees' public pension insurance according to the country's unification policies, allowing a certain differences among different regions and enterprises. In 1993, the principle of "social pooling and individual retirement account (SP & IRA)" was first proposed. In March 1995, the State Council promulgated "Announcement on Deepening the Reform of Pension Insurance System for Enterprise Employees" which clearly put forward that the reform direction of China's public pension insurance system for urban employees was the implementation of a combination of social pooling and individual retirement account.

In July 1997, the State Council promulgated the "Decisions on the Establishment of a Unified Enterprise Employees' Basic Pension Insurance System", then the system of basic pension insurance

---

2   As regards the increase of Chinese public pension expenditures, please also see Figure 3-4 and Figure 3-5.

3   In 2014, the state council decided to combine the two social pension insurance systems for urban and rural residents.

4   The system of basic pension insurance for urban employees is a mandatory public insurance system set up for urban employees thereby it is also called "public pension insurance system for urban employees".

for urban employees based on the pattern of social pooling and individual retirement account (SP & IRA) had been formally established which reflected the combination of equity and efficiency. Since 1997, China had moved from an enterprise-based system of defined benefit pensions based on final salary toward a unified system for urban workers.

The greatest contribution of this "Decisions" was to integrate public pension insurance system for urban employees in China and to adhere to the reform direction of the public pension insurance system for urban employees which combined social pooling and individual retirement account. "Decisions" issued by the State Council in 1997 confirmed the basic pattern of the current public pension insurance system for urban employees and played a great role in terms of expanding the coverage of the system. By the end of 1997, the number of people who participated in basic pension insurance for urban employees was 112.04 million (86.71 and 25.33 million for employees and retirees separately), climbed up to 136.17 million by the end of 2000 (104.47 and 31.70 million for employees and retirees separately), with the annual average growth rate of 6.72%, while rose to 257.07 million by the end of 2010 (194.02 and 63.05 million for employees and retirees separately), with the annual average growth rate of 6.56%. By the end of 2014, the number of people covered by the basic pension insurance for urban employees had been up to 341.24 million (255.31 and 85.93 million for employees and retirees separately).

In July 2011, the pilot reform of social pension insurance for urban residents was launched. According to "Guidelines on Implementation of Pilot of Social Pension Insurance for Urban Residents" issued by the State Council, the urban residents who were 16 years old and above, were not employed and were ineligible to basic pension insurance for urban employees had been covered in the range of public pension insurance system. In 2011 the scope of the pilot across the country covered 60% of the regions and aimed to basically achieve full coverage in 2012.

By the end of 2011, 1902 counties (cities, districts, banners) in 27 provinces (autonomous regions) and some districts and counties in 4 centrally administered municipalities had carried out the pilot reform of new rural social pension insurance. By the end of 2011 the number of participants of social pension insurance for urban residents was 5.39 million. The fund revenue of social pension insurance for urban residents was 4 billion yuan with 6 hundred million yuan of individual contributions. The amount of fund expenditures was 1.1 billion yuan and the accumulated balance was 3.2 billion yuan.

(2) Pilot of Rural Public Pension System

Since the reform and opening up, a great number of rural labor forces migrated to urban area. This kind of migration resulted in gradually serious population aging in rural area. With the young rural labor forces moving towards urban area, the traditional function of rural family security had also weakened.

On the other hand, with the transition of rural population structure, the general reduction of the land that household contracted for, and the growth of the land which was requisitioned and developed, the security function of the land had weakened constantly. More and more rural older persons could not depend on the land for their old-age support. Traditionally, old-age support of rural people was based on their own families. The role and function of the state and government for the old-age support of the rural older persons was not distinct.

In September 2009, the State Council issued "Guidelines on the Implementation of the Pilot of New Rural Social Pension Insurance" and decided to carry out the pilot reform of new rural social pension insurance since 2009. In accordance with this "Guidelines", Chinese rural residents could enjoy the national pension system of generalized preference after the age of 60-year-old. The benefit of new rural social pension insurance was composed of basic pension and the individual account pension.[5]

The amount of the per capita monthly basic pension which was confirmed by the central government was 55 yuan. Based on the actual situations, the local government might increase the standard of the basic pension. The per capita monthly basic pension was entirely contributed by the central public finance. New rural social pension insurance had also clarified the subsidy responsibility of the local government to the pension insurance contributions of the rural residents and formulated the specific subsidy amount of the local government to the contributions of rural pension insurance participants. This indicated that the financing and security pattern of pension insurance of Chinese rural residents had undergone the significant changes. The responsibility of the state and government for achievement of "the elderly should receive proper caregiving" had been emphasized and demonstrated.

The pilot reform of new rural social pension insurance had made significant progress. By the end of 2011, 1914 counties (cities, districts, banners) in 27 provinces (autonomous regions) and some districts and counties in 4 centrally administered municipalities had carried out the pilot reform of new rural social pension insurance.

(3) Combination of Pension Insurance System for Urban and Rural Residents

The basic pension insurance for urban and rural residents is based on the new rural social pension insurance and social pension insurance for urban residents. In 2014, the State Council decided to combine the new rural social pension insurance and social pension insurance for urban residents to set up the nationally unified basic pension insurance for urban and rural residents. By the end of 2014, the number of people who had been covered by the basic pension insurance for urban and rural residents was 501 million.

3 Public Pension Arrangements

At present, the current public pension scheme is composed of two different pillars: basic pension insurance for urban employees, and basic pension insurance for urban and rural residents. In 1997, with the integration of China's public pension insurance for urban employees, the basic pattern of social pooling and individual retirement account (SP & IRA) had been formally established. The pilot reform of new rural social pension insurance and social pension insurance for urban residents was launched in 2009 and 2011 respectively. In 2014, the state council decided to combine both of these two pension insurance systems to set up basic pension insurance for urban and rural residents.

---

5   In the study, "basic pension" refers to the one part of benefits that the beneficiaries or pensioners achieve, whereas the other part is "individual account pension" that is accumulated in the individual retirement account.

3.1 Basic Pension Insurance for Urban Employees

China's public pension system for urban employees is the mandatory "basic pension insurance system" which provides the pension insurance participants with the basic living security after their retirement. The system of basic pension insurance for urban employees is based on combination of the social pooling and individual retirement account. The state, enterprises and individuals share the burden of pension insurance financing. In terms of social pooling, the pension insurance is financed by the state and the enterprises, whereas the enterprises and individuals should contribute to the individual retirement account with different contribution rate.

Social pooling and individual retirement account (SP & IRA) means that the public pension insurance system for urban employees is composed of both social pooling and individual retirement account. "Decisions on the Establishment of a Unified Enterprise Employees' Basic Pension Insurance System" promulgated by the State Council in July 1997 specified that each enterprise must pay contribution fees of pension insurance for their employees both to the social pooling fund and also to the individual retirement account. The employees must contribute to their individual retirement accounts during the course of their employment. The total contribution rate of the enterprises should not normally exceed 20%. The contribution rate that employees contribute to their individual accounts starts from 4% and increases by 1% every two years ultimately reaching 8%. With the growth of the contribution rate of employees' individual retirement accounts the contribution rate of the enterprises to the individual retirement accounts should decline correspondingly from 7% to 3%. That is, the total contribution rate of individual retirement account from both the enterprises and employees should be up to 11%. The benefits include both the basic pension from the social pooling fund and the pension from individual retirement account. Since January 1 2006, the magnitude of individual retirement account has been unified from 11% to 8% of the employees' contribution wages which is entirely from individual contributions. The contributions from the enterprises have no longer been included in the individual retirement account.

For those employees whose individual contributions accumulated over 15 years, the monthly basic

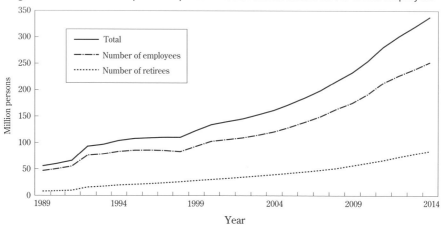

Figure 3-3. Number of People Participated in Basic Pension Insurance for Urban Employees

Source: *China Statistical Yearbook 2015*, National Bureau of Statistics of China.

pension has been paid after the retirement. The benefits of pension include basic pension and individual account pension. The standard of the basic pension is the 20% of the average monthly wage of the employees for the last year and the standard of the individual account pension is the amount of the individual account divided by 139.

By the end of 2014, the number of pension insurance participants had reached 341.24 million including 255.31 million employees and 85.93 million retirees (Figure 3-3).

As shown in Figure 3-4, the revenue, expense and balance of basic pension insurance fund in the recent decades had increased greatly and very fast. Compared with those in 2000, the revenue and expense of basic pension insurance fund in 2010 had increased by 4 or 5 times. By the end of 2014, revenue of basic pension insurance fund had been up to 27,620 hundred million yuan, and accumulated

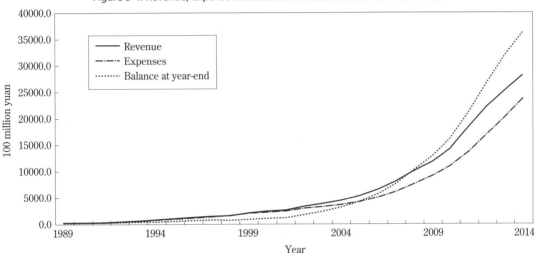

Figure 3-4. Revenue, Expense and Balance of Basic Pension Insurance Fund

Source: *China Statistical Yearbook 2015*, National Bureau of Statistics of China.

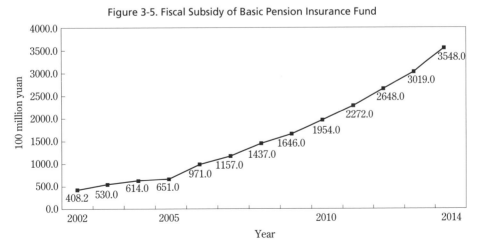

Figure 3-5. Fiscal Subsidy of Basic Pension Insurance Fund

Source: *Communiqué on the Statistics of Humam Resoucs and Social Security Development 2002-2014*, Ministry of Human Resources and Social Security.

balance of basic pension insurance fund was 35,645 hundred million yuan. In 2002, the fiscal subsidy of basic pension insurance fund was 408 hundred million yuan, whereas by the end of 2014, the amount had climbed up to 3,548 hundred million yuan (Figure 3-5).

3.2 Basic Pension Insurance for Urban and Rural Residents

The predecessor of basic pension insurance for urban and rural residents is the new rural social pension insurance and social pension insurance for urban residents. On September 1 2009, the State Council issued "Guidelines on New Rural Social Pension Insurance Pilot" to determine the basic principles of new rural social pension insurance as well as financing patterns, coverage of insurance, accounting policies and administration system. Then the pilot was officially launched in the some regions of the whole country. By the end of 2009, the pilot proposals of new rural social pension insurance had been approved in 320 pilot counties (cities, districts, banners) of 27 provinces (autonomous regions) and four centrally administered municipalities.

Since 2011, urban residents who are 16 years old and above, are not employed and are ineligible to basic pension insurance for urban employees have been covered in the range of public pension insurance system.

On February 2014, the State Council decided to combine the new rural social pension insurance and social pension insurance for urban residents to set up the nationally unified basic pension insurance for urban and rural residents. By the end of 2014, the number of participants of basic pension insurance for urban and rural residents had been 501 million. The fund revenue of basic pension insurance for urban and rural residents was 231 billion yuan with 67 billion individual contributions. The amount of fund expenditures was 157 billion yuan and the accumulated balance was 385 billion yuan.

(1) Basic Principles

The basic principle of basic pension insurance for urban and rural residents is "overall coverage, basic security, flexibility and sustainability". Individuals (households) and the government have the reasonable sharing of responsibilities, with rights corresponding to obligations. By the end of "the 12th Five-Year Plan" period, the combination of the new rural social pension insurance and social pension insurance for urban residents, and its integration with basic pension insurance for urban employees would basically achieve in China.

(2) Financing Patterns

Basic pension insurance for urban and rural residents is financed by combination of individual contributions, collective subsidies and government subsidies. The urban and rural residents who have been 16 years old (and have not been educated in the schools) and have not been covered by basic pension insurance for urban employees are eligible to participate in basic pension insurance system for urban and rural residents.

The urban and rural residents who participate in basic pension insurance system for urban and rural residents have to contribute to the pension insurance according to the policies. The annual amount of per capita individual contributions is divided by twelve levels, 100 yuan, 200 yuan, 300 yuan, 400 yuan,

500 yuan, 600 yuan, 700 yuan, 800 yuan, 900 yuan, 1,000 yuan, 1,500 yuan and 2,000 yuan. The local government may increase the level of contributions based on the actual situations. The pension insurance participants are voluntary to choose the contribution level with "more contributions, more benefits".

Village collectives who have better financial capacity should be responsible for the contribution subsidies of the pension insurance participants. The village meetings held by the village committee determine the subsidy standards democratically. The state encourages other sources of financing including social organizations, other economic organizations, as well as the personal fund for contributions of pension insurance participants.

The local government pays subsidies to the contribution fees of pensioners. The annual amount of the per capita contribution subsidies of local government is no less than 30 yuan. It is encouraged to choose a higher standard of contribution fee, with the specific criteria and policies decided by the provincial (district and municipal) government. For those severely disabled and other disadvantaged groups, the local government provides the partial or full payment of the pension fee at the minimum level.

The individual contributions of urban and rural residents, the contribution subsidies of the local government, and other funds for contributions have totally been in the individual account which is accumulated in the real account.

(3) Benefits

The benefits of basic pension insurance for urban and rural residents involve the basic pension and the individual account pension. The urban and rural participants in the pension insurance who have been 60 years old and eligible to the relative requirements may receive the basic pension.

The central government has the responsibility to confirm the minimum standards of the basic pension insurance and to establish the normal adjustment mechanism of minimum standards of basic pension insurance. The local government may increase the standard based on the actual situations. For those who perform long-term payment of pension contributions, the local government has rights to raise the amount of the basic pension and has the responsibility for the payment of this extra sum of pension fund.

The monthly pension benefit of individual retirement account is the amount that the total amount of individual account is divided by 139 (the same as that of current basic pension insurance for urban employees). If the pensioners die, the balance of the individual account excluding the government subsidies could be legally inherited.

(4) The Eligible Requirement for Benefits

The age enjoying the benefits of basic pension insurance for urban and rural residents is 60 years old for both male and female residents. At the time when the new rural social pension insurance and social pension insurance for urban residents implemented, those who had been 60 years old and above and had not been covered by basic pension insurance for urban employees or other public pension system did not have to contribute to the pension insurance, whereas they might receive a monthly basic pension; for those who had less than 15 years away from the age receiving the benefits, they should perform the annual contributions with the supplementary contributions permitted. The accumulated years for contributions were no more than 15 years. For those who have more than 15 years away from the age receiving the benefits, they should perform the annual contributions with the accumulated years for contributions no less than 15 years.

4　Features of Public Pension System

4.1　SP & IRA and PAYG

Basic pension insurance for urban employees is constructed in the forms of social pooling and individual retirement account (SP & IRA) which is financed on a Pay-As-You-Go (PAYG) basis.

As for basic pension insurance for urban and rural residents, there is no "social pooling", alternatively, the basic pension which is fully financed by the government has been set up. In addition, the government sets up the individual account of pension insurance for each participant for their lifelong pension records.

As regards financing, pension plans can be classified into fully funded, partially funded, or PAYG scheme. In a fully funded scheme, the contribution rate is chosen so as to accumulate a stock of capital that, at any point in time, should equal the present discounted value of future benefits minus future contributions of those currently in the scheme. In a PAYG scheme, benefits accruing to the current beneficiaries are financed by current contributions or budget transfers. A partially funded scheme combines features of a fully funded and a PAYG scheme (but where reserves do not fully meet the aforementioned financial condition). A defined-contribution plan is usually fully funded. Defined-benefit plans, on the other hand, are most often organized as either PAYG or partially funded.

Public pension scheme in China is financed on a PAYG basis. Since the State Council promulgated the "Decisions on the Establishment of a Unified Enterprise Employees' Basic Pension Insurance System" in July 1997, each locality in China started to establish a unified public pension system based on SP & IRA. The original intention of the establishment of this public pension system for urban employees is to make it gradually get rid of PAYG scheme with the accumulating functions of individual retirement account and to transfer to the partially funded system. In the context of the actual operation situation, however, the functions which help the transitions of financing pattern have not emerged although the individual retirement account has played a role in attracting and encouraging employees to contribute. The reason is probably that the individual retirement account in most regions of China is the "empty account" which is lack of real fund in the account.

4.2　Financing Responsibility of the Government

In the pilot reform of social pension insurance for urban residents and new rural social pension insurance, the financing responsibility of the government has been reinforced greatly. At the same time, the multi-financing pattern has also been confirmed. In terms of the financing pattern and financing responsibility, actually social pension insurance for urban residents is nearly the same as new rural social pension insurance. This type of financing pattern has confirmed the subsidy responsibility of the central and local public finance which invests sustainable subsidy fund. Basic pension insurance for urban employees which has already implemented for a couple of years is not financed by the stable financing resources such as the public finance but with a number of special subsidies to offset the financial gap. Significantly the efficiency of the implementation is much lower.

(1) Social Pension Insurance for Urban Residents

It should be clearly implemented that the local government provided subsidies for contribution fees and the central government provided subsidies for the basic pension benefits. In accordance with the guidance opinions of the State Council, the central public finance is responsible for the subsidy for the basis pension, and the local public finance is responsible for the individual contribution subsidy of people who participate in social pension insurance for urban residents.

(2) New Rural Social Pension Insurance

In light of old rural social pension insurance,[6] in which the rural residents have to pay for their own contribution fees, actually it was a mode of self-saving. While the most significant feature of new rural social pension insurance is the establishment of a new financing pattern which combines the individual contribution, collective subsidies and the government subsidies. Compared with the system of old rural social pension insurance which set up the individual account for rural residents, new rural social pension insurance was built on the basis of basic pension and individual retirement account. In particular, the central public finance provides the rural residents with the subsidies directly. There are two parts of benefits: basic pension and individual accounts pension. The basic pension is subsidized totally by the central public finance. This means that rural residents would enjoy the national pension insurance of generalized-preference after the age of 60-year-old. According to the plan it will be the year of 2020 to realize that all of the rural residents would be entitled to social pension insurance.

4.3 "Real Account" of Basic Pension Insurance for Urban and Rural Residents

The individual retirement account of basic pension insurance for urban and rural residents is implemented with "real account" to guarantee the safety of the fund. The individual contribution fees, the contribution subsidies of the local government, collective subsidies and other sources of contribution subsidies are all credited to individual retirement account. The fund of individual retirement account is counted for interest based on the bank one-year deposit interest rates. Other uses of individual retirement account fund are not permitted. This type of individual retirement account is essentially different from that of basic pension insurance for urban employees which has to continue to pay pensions for those "old" people who had already retired when the basic pension insurance was implemented and has to accumulate the pension fund for those "new" people who just participate in the pension insurance system. The appearance of "empty account" is inevitable during the transitions from the PAYG to "partially or fully funded" system. At the beginning, it is confirmed that the system of "real account" is

---

6   Here the system of old rural social pension insurance refers to social pension insurance system in rural China that was implemented before the pilot of new rural social pension insurance was launched.

conducted in which the fund is credited to the individual as the bank savings, therefore the attractiveness of the system is enhanced. Obviously, it is the most critical issue to maintain and increase the value of the individual retirement account fund in order to achieve the sustainability of individual retirement account.

4.4 Diversity of Basic Pension Insurance for Urban and Rural Residents

A certain diversity exist in terms of the system design of basic pension insurance for urban and rural residents which is corresponding to the financial capabilities of different groups of residents. The diversity of the system means that to the great extent, it realizes the wide coverage on the premise of residents' voluntary participation in the system. The annual amount of per capita contributions of basic pension insurance for urban and rural residents includes 12 levels which are from 100 yuan to 2,000 yuan.

The principles of "voluntary choices of contribution levels" and "more contributions, more benefits" conform to the situation of different financial capability of the pension insurance participants and also respect the personal preferences and requirements for the pension security. Meanwhile, it is permitted that the local government develop appropriate supporting measures according to the actual situation, such as increasing the subsidy standards of the local government, enhancing the contribution levels, raising the amount of the subsidy for those participants who have contributed more to the system. All of these policies which have taken into account the unbalance development all over the country are helpful to improve the local initiatives.

5　Reform of Public Pension System

Before the 1980s, in the context of the young demographic structure and the planned economy, public pension insurance system for urban employees was the generation-transferred system with the enterprises as the risk-scattered units. With the transitions from a planned economy to a market economy system and the arrival of population aging society, the overall reform of the public pension system had initiated since 1991. The pattern of social pooling and individual retirement account (SP & IRA) was proposed for first time in 1993. Social pooling and individual retirement account (SP & IRA) which was officially established in 1997 was of great significance with the equity and efficiency combined. On the basis of the reform practices in recent years, the system has played a certain role to solve the unfair competition among enterprises. The individual responsibility of this system has been strengthened step by step. Therefore the system is moving towards the intended direction. However, some problems concerning the implementation of the system exist. The system is confronted with the crisis that poses a huge challenge to the sustainable development of the current system. At present, the individual retirement account is actually a system of PAYG rather than partially or fully funded. The system which is financed exclusively or partially on a PAYG basis is particularly vulnerable to population aging. On the other hand, social pension insurance for urban residents and new rural social pension insurance which had been combined in 2014 require further reform.

5.1 Extending Retirement Ages

The retirement age is an essential factor in determining the level of pension burden. One of the options frequently considered is to delay the age at which employees become eligible for beneficiaries. This approach has been undertaken by several countries, most notably the United States, which will gradually extend the normal retirement age at which a full pension is received for both men and women. Given that the average life expectancy of the population and the security level are constant, the average years of enjoying the pension reduce if the retirement age increases, then the total burden of the pension alleviate. The ILO study showed that extending the retirement age can result in the significant effect that pension income increase and pension expenditure decrease. For example, pension expenditure would increase by 50% if the retirement age reduces from 65 to 60 years old. According to projection of Chinese experts, the pension fund of social pooling in China would increase by 4 billion yuan, reducing expenditure by 16 billion yuan, mitigating the fund gap by 20 billion yuan if the retirement age is extended for one additional year. As a result, the extension of retirement age plays a greatly important role to ease crisis of pension payments. It is necessary for China to gradually increase the retirement age which should be guaranteed in conformity with legal provisions.

5.2 Eliminating Transfer Costs

We need to widely explore a variety of funding channels through various approaches including: (1) Reducing state-owned shares of which the income is placed into the pension insurance fund to cover the gap. In June 2001, The State Council issued an "Interim Procedure on Reduction of State-owned Shares and the Administration of Financing Social Security Fund" which needs to be improved in terms of the operability and enforcement at present; (2) Levy of specific taxes. The specific taxes including inheritance tax, gift tax, special consumption tax or a special social insurance tax can be specifically used to offset the pension insurance fund gap; (3) Issuing social security bonds so as to finance hidden liabilities. Thereby with the approaches of a special tax, this part of the bonds could be cashed gradually in the long run and the problem of hidden liabilities would be ultimately solved; (4) Increasing the central financial transfer payment, and mainly making up for insufficiency of basic pension insurance fund in the less developed area.

5.3 Reducing Average Replacement Rates[7]

Another approach to be considered is that of reducing the average replacement rate, thereby lowering in one step the benefits enjoyed by pensioners as a proportion of average wages. According to the projection and estimation by IMF, the pension replacement rate of major industrial countries was 37.5% in 1995, 37.1% in 2000, 35.4% in 2010 and 35.8% in 2030. In Germany, France and Italy, the rate was much

---

7 The replacement rate is defined as the average monthly pension benefit as a percentage of average gross wage of on-the-job employees last year when the pensioners are eligible to apply for retirement.

higher up to 50-60%, whereas in Japan the rate was below 20%.[8]

In 2005, the average replacement rate of enterprises in China was 49.3%.[9] Based on the current economic development of China it is preferred to set the average replacement rate of no more than 50%. Lower average replacement rate can greatly reduce the pressure on the payment of pension fund and provide the necessary possibilities for development of enterprise supplementary pension insurance and pension insurance of individual savings to establish a truly multi-pillar pension insurance system. Reducing average replacement rates can enhance the initiative of enterprises to participate in the public pension insurance system and to further extend the coverage of the system.

5.4   Expanding the Coverage of Public Pension Insurance System

The employees in urban privately-owned and self-employment enterprises as well as foreign-funded enterprises should be included in the public pension insurance system to expand the coverage of the system and to reduce the system dependency ratio.[10] For those state-owned enterprises which are unable to pay the contribution, the state should disburse in the state budget or share the responsibilities in proportion to the central or local budget.

5.5   Setting Up Independent Accounts

Implementation of independent accounts for both social pooling fund and individual retirement account fund would prevent the individual retirement account fund from being possessed or diverted for other purpose. Thus it is helpful to establish "real account". In terms of properties, the social pooling fund is different from the individual retirement account fund. In essence, it is required to perform the separate management of fund. Social pooling is conducted with the type of PAYG system which is absolute transfer payments without problems of fund accumulation and maintenance and increment of the value. The principal issue of management is the full contribution and payment of fund on time on which the existing social insurance agency could perform the unified management. The individual retirement account is conducted with the type of saving accumulation system. Pension fund accumulated in the individual retirement account is confronted with the problems of value maintenance and increment due to the effect of inflation and wage growth rate. The major task of management is to how to achieve the specific security, profitability and liquidity of the fund. The individual retirement account fund which has the nature of fully-funded-scheme should be administrated by the dependent agency. The focus of management is the investment and operations of the fund.

---

8   Chand, S. K., Jaeger, A. (1996) *Aging Populations and Public Pension Schemes,* Washington D.C.: International Monetary Fund, Occasional Paper, p.12.

9   Ministry of Human Resources and Social Security, 2005.

10   The system dependency ratio is defined as the ratio of retirees to the on-the-job employees both of whom are covered by public pension insurance system. In the context of PAYG system, the ratio reflects the number of older persons (beneficiaries) that the employees (contributors) have to support.

5.6 Guaranteeing Financing Resources

It is necessary to guarantee the financing resources of basic pension insurance for urban and rural residents. It is necessary to encourage the individual contributions and secure the government subsidies. It is essential to set up the financing pattern that individual contributions, collective subsidies and government subsidies combined and to guarantee the financing resources of collective subsidies and government subsidies.

In order to ensure the effective operation and sustainable development of basic pension insurance for urban and rural residents, the local rural collective economic organizations who had better financial capability should provide a certain proportion of contribution subsidies for rural residents. The local government should provide some fund subsidies based on the local financial capacity for those participants. In the context of pilot implementation all over the whole country, the fund subsides of the local government play great importance in both developed regions and developing regions.

5.7 Promoting Integration of Urban-Rural System

It is necessary to explore effective approaches to improve the integration of different public pension insurance systems. The local government should also get rid of the rural-urban segmentation system to explore the measures of basic pension transfer between urban and rural areas and to gradually establish and improve public pension insurance system which covers both the urban and rural residents.

5.8 Promoting Transfer and Integration of Different Systems

In order to meet the needs of different groups, China have built up various forms of public pension insurance systems which had played a positive role to solve the problems of old-age support. In recent years, however, the institutional arrangements which are fragmented have seriously hindered the connections between different systems. As a new type of pension insurance arrangement, basic pension insurance for urban and rural residents may have to confront the transfer and integration with other pension insurance system. In practice, basic pension insurance for urban and rural residents should be reinforced for the transfer and integration with the new rural social pension insurance system and basic pension insurance for urban employees. On February 24 2014, the Ministry of Human Resources and Social Security, and the Ministry of Finance issued "Measures on the Connection of Urban-rural Pension Insurance Systems" which was implemented on July 1 2014. It was the first time to clearly confirm the possibility of transfer and connection for the two pension systems-Basic pension insurance for urban and rural residents, and basic pension insurance for urban employees.

References

Bonoli, G., Shinkawa, T. (ed.) (2005) *Ageing and pension reform around the world: evidence from eleven countries,* Edward Elgar Publishing Limited.

Cai, X. (2011) *Research on the Sustainability of Basic Endowment Insurance System with SP & IRA for Urban Employment in China,* Economic Science Press.

Chand, S. K., Jaeger, A. (1996) *Aging Populations and Public Pension Schemes,* Washington D.C.: International Monetary Fund, Occasional Paper.

Deng, D. -S., Xue, H. (2010) "Study on the Issues in the Conduction and Process of the New Rural Public Pension Scheme" *Reform of Economic System* 1, pp.86-92.

Liu, C. -P. (2008) "Introspection and Reconstruction of Chinese 'Social Pooling with Individual Account' Public Pension System" *The Theory and Practice of Finance and Economics* 29 (155), pp.26-30.

World Bank. (1997) *Old Age Security: China 2020,* Washington D.C.

Zheng, G. (2011) *The Strategy of Social Security System in China,* Renmin Press.

Chapter 4

An Empirical Analysis of the Incidence of Employers' Contributions to Health Care and Long-Term Care Insurance in Japan

Naomi Miyazato and Seiritsu Ogura

1 Introduction

In the last two decades, social insurance taxes for health care and long-term care in Japan have been raised repeatedly in order to finance the increasing costs of caring for the country's aging population. Almost all the laws governing social insurance programs for employed workers in Japan mandate that firms contribute at least one-half of social insurance taxes, leaving the remainder to be paid by employees. However, the employers' contributions could be shifted so that more of the burden is be borne by the workers. This effect of the law on the relative tax burden of employers and employees is known as the incidence of social insurance taxes. As we will see below, the incidence of social insurance taxes on wages or salaries depends theoretically on the price elasticity of the demand and supply of labor. Thus the question how much of past increases in social insurance taxes have been shifted to labor is mainly an empirical one. However, most previous studies focused on the effects of these taxes on the wages and employment of regular workers only.

Figure 4-1 shows the changes in the social security taxes and wage rates of regular and non-regular workers in Japan since the mid-1980s. The burden of social insurance taxes has been increasing throughout this period, with the wage rates of both regular and non-regular workers increasing steadily until the early 1990s. While both wage rates increased slightly during the 1990s, the wage rates of regular workers decreased and the wage rates of non-regular workers increased steadily during the 2000s. In addition, according to the Labor Force Survey[1] conducted by the Ministry of Health, Labor and Welfare, the number of regular workers reached its peak in 1997 at 38.1 million; the number has decreased steadily since then and was 33.6 million in 2010. In contrast, the number of non-regular workers has been increasing steadily, from 6.04 million in 1984 to 8.8 million in 1990, 12.7 million in 2000, and 17.6 million in 2010.

In Japan, non-regular workers are not covered by corporate-based social insurance taxes, as will be explained below. If the employers' cost savings from hiring more non-regular workers exceeds resultant productivity loss, the employers will have an incentive to hire more non-regular workers in place of regular workers. Therefore, in this paper, we investigate the wage rates not only of regular workers but also of non-regular workers when analyzing the effect of social insurance programs. In addition, we use micro data for the wages and salaries to estimate the incidence. The remainder of this paper is structured as follows: In Section 2, we review preceding studies. In Section 3, we explain the institutional

---

1   For more information about the survey, please see http://www.stat.go.jp/english/data/roudou/.

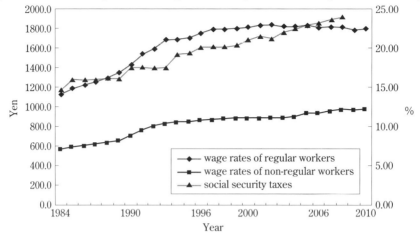

Figure 4-1. Social Security Taxes and Wage Rates of Regular and Non-Regular Workers in Japan

Note: Social security taxes are the summation of employees' pension premiums, average premiums of society-managed employment-based health insurance programs, and average premiums of LTCI programs. Social security taxes were not levied on annual special earnings before 2003. We recalculated the annual special earnings with the social security taxes levied.

Source: Basic Survey on Wage Structure, Ministry of Health, Labor and Welfare (http://www.mhlw.go.jp/english/database/db-l/wage-structure.html): Social Security Statistical Yearbook, National Institute of Population and Social Security Research (http://www.ipss.go.jp/s-toukei/j/t_nenpo_back/libr_new.html).

background. In Section 4, we explain our empirical specifications and the nature of our data. In Section 5, we present our estimation results. Finally, in Section 6, we summarize the paper.

2 Preceding Studies

According to a standard economic theory, the incidence of employers' contributions to social insurance depends on the elasticity of the demand and supply curves. There are a significant number of studies on the incidence of employers' contributions in the United States and European countries. For example, Brittain (1971), Vroman (1974), and Holmlund (1983) analyzed the effect of social insurance taxes on wages and employment using aggregated data. According to these studies, almost all, or at least half, of the employers' social insurance contributions are shifted to the employees in the form of reduced wage rates. In the 1990s, micro data were used to avoid endogeneity bias, and many studies began to rely on the exogenous changes that occurred in social insurance contributions as a result of reforms in social insurance programs. Such studies include Gruber and Krueger (1991), Gruber (1994, 1997), and Anderson and Meyer (2000); most of them confirmed the shifting of employers' contributions to the workers. Most recently, Sommers (2005) analyzed the incidence problem in the presence of wage rigidity.

However, it is also possible that employers replace their full-time workers with part-time workers when their social insurance taxes are increased because social insurance taxes are not levied on part-time workers. Baicker and Chandra (2006) analyzed whether rising health insurance premiums would

Chapter 4 An Empirical Analysis of the Incidence of Employers' Contributions to Health Care and Long-Term Care Insurance in Japan

decrease the wage rates of full-time workers and increase the employment opportunities of part-time workers. Their results show that an increase in health insurance premiums does lead to an increase in the probability of employing part-time workers. The importance of substituting full-time workers with part-time workers is also mentioned in Thurston (1997).

In Japan, among the limited number of empirical studies on this issue are Komamura and Yamada (2004), Iwamoto and Hamaaki (2006), Sakai and Kazekami (2007), Tachibanaki and Yokoyama (2008), and Hamaaki and Iwamoto (2010). Tachibanaki and Yokoyama (2008), on the one hand, analyzed the macro time-series data of social insurance taxes and wages, found no statistically significant negative correlation between them, and concluded that social insurance taxes are not shifted to workers. On the other hand, Komamura and Yamada (2004) analyzed the data of (corporate-based) health insurance associations and found that major portions of the employers' contributions are shifted to workers in the form of reduced wages. Iwamoto and Hamaaki (2006) indicated that the results of existing Japanese studies are susceptible to the endogeneity bias of employers' contributions. Hamaaki and Iwamoto (2010) indicated that the burden of social insurance is shifted back to employees to some extent. Sakai and Kazekami (2007) used aggregated data to analyze the incidence problem, taking advantage of the introduction of the Long-Term Care Insurance (LTCI) program in 2000 as their natural experiment. They found that after the LTCI was introduced, relative wages of male workers who had to pay for the insurance declined, possibly because the employers shifted LTCI contributions to the workers. However, these studies in Japan looked only at the wages of full-time workers.

3 Institutional Backgrounds

In this section, we briefly explain the health care and LTCI programs in Japan (Figure 4-2). First, health care insurance is compulsory and universal, built on occupational and regional bases. Occupation-based insurance falls into three categories: (1) government-managed insurance, (2) society-managed insurance, (3) and mutual aid associations. Regional insurance, on the other hand, is managed by the municipal government. Whereas employers must legally contribute to their employees' health care insurance under occupation-based insurances, there is no employer contribution in regional-based insurance. In this paper, we focus on occupation-based insurance because we investigate the incidence of employer's contributions. Moreover, there are two types of occupation-based insurance, one for small-size firms and the other for large-size firms or associations-that is, those with more 700 employees or more than 3,000 associate members. Government-managed insurance corresponds to the former insurance type, while society-managed insurance and mutual aid associations correspond to the latter type. In government-managed insurance, the contributions of employers and employees must be equal, that is, 50% to 50%. For example, if the health care insurance rate is 8.2% of wages, employers contribute 4.1% and employees 4.1%. However, in society-managed insurance and mutual aid associations, the employers' share can be higher than the employees' share, and therefore, employers' contributions are varied. We use these variations to analyze the incidence of employers' contributions. Self-employed workers,

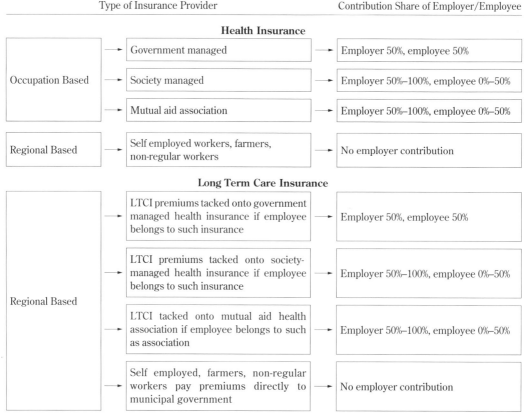

Figure 4-2. Overview of Health and Long-Term Care Insurance in Japan

farmers, and non-regular workers, who are not covered by occupation-based health insurance, must therefore enroll in regional-based health insurance programs. There is no employers' contribution in these programs.

LTCI was introduced in 2000 and is managed on a regional basis. However, because insurance contributions under this program are tacked onto health care insurance contributions, the collection schemes and the manner in which employers contribute to LTCI are the same as for health care insurance. The contributions of employers and employees under the LTCI are equal, that is, 50%-50%, just as under government-managed health insurance programs. Under society-managed insurance programs and mutual aid associations, employers' contributions for employees can exceed 50%. In addition, there is no employers' contribution for self-employed workers, farmers, or non-regular workers. We also use variations in employers' contributions under the LTCI for our analysis of the incidence of employers' contributions. However, there is a difference between the LTCI and health care insurance schemes. Although no LTCI contributions are levied for workers under the age of 40, health care insurance contributions are levied for them, so that employers need not contribute to the LTCI for those workers. We use this institutional difference in the difference-in-difference (DID) estimation. Moreover, persons over age 65 receive long-term care benefits under the LTCI, but those under 65 do not.

Finally, we examine the case of non-regular workers, who are not covered by occupation-based

Chapter 4 An Empirical Analysis of the Incidence of Employers' Contributions to Health Care and Long-Term Care Insurance in Japan   **65**

social insurance programs. They must contribute to regional-based insurance programs, managed by municipal governments, and hence employers do not have to contribute to their insurance. Non-regular workers can be defined as: (1) those who work fewer than three-fourth the normal working hours of full-time workers per day or per week, or (2) those whose working days in one month are fewer than three-fourth the normal working days of full-time workers. If the cost savings of the employers from hiring more non-regular workers exceed their resultant productivity loss, employers are likely to hire more non-regular workers in place of regular workers. We therefore investigate employers' contributions and the wages of non-regular workers in addition to that of regular workers.

4   Estimation Model and Data

4.1   Estimation Model

We empirically analyze the incidence of employers' contributions to health care insurance and LTCI by using large-scale national microdata on wages from what is known as the Employment Status Survey (1992, 1997, and 2002). We also use the information on society-managed health insurance programs from the Annual Business Report of the National Federation of Health Insurance Societies (1992, 1997, and 2002). In the Japanese empirical literature, all the previous studies relied on aggregated wage data, but as far as we know, none of them used micro data. By using a large-scale national micro data set for wages, we can expect to obtain more precise estimates of the incidence of social insurance fees or taxes, since we can control the attributes of individual workers and characteristics of the firms, regions, and industries more precisely. We use a standard specification of the wage equation given as follows:

$$\ln w_{i,t} = \beta_0 + X_{i,t}\beta + \gamma_1 \tau_{j,t} + \varepsilon_{i,t} \tag{1}$$

where w_i is the wage rate of worker i; $\ln w_i$ the logarithm of w_i, and β_0 the constant term. A vector X_i stands for individual attributes such as age, sex, education, size of the workforce, industry, and region, and τ_j is the employers' contribution rate for social insurance, including those for health and long-term care of the jth industry. The subscript t denotes time. If the coefficient γ_1 has a negative sign in the regular worker wage equation, we can conclude that the employers' contributions to the social insurance schemes are shifted to the employees. In the Employment Status Survey (1992, 1997, and 2002) that we use, we have information about the industry, the classification of firms by the size of their total employment, and the regions where the firms are located, but not about the firms' identities. As a result, instead of using individual employers' contribution rates for health care insurance and LTCI programs, we computed the weighted average of these firm contribution rates for each industry in each region, using the number of regular workers of individual firms as weights. The computed average rate for the firms of a given industry in a given region is used as the contribution rate as τ_j in the estimated equations. Since we have wage data for regular workers as well as non-regular workers, we estimate the wage equations separately using identical specification. As we have mentioned above, γ_1 in the regular worker wage equation shows the standard incidence. The same variable in the non-regular worker wage equation, however, departs from the standard model; there is no employers' contribution to social insurance programs for them. Therefore, employers have an incentive to replace regular workers with non-regular workers if the cost savings from not having to pay employers' contributions is greater than the productivity losses possibly caused by having a greater number of non-regular workers. Replacing regular workers with non-regular workers leads to increased demand for non-regular workers. Thus, the coefficient γ_1 in the non-regular worker wage equation is expected to be positive.

Next, we employ DID estimations to analyze the incidence of employers' contribution to social security programs. If there is a correlation between the employers' contribution rate τ and error term ε owing to unobserved heterogeneity such as a worker's ability, the ordinary least squares (OLS) estimation of Equation (1) will have a bias. Social insurance rates in society-based insurance and mutual aid associations are determined by each firm or association. Able workers are likely to work at firms that provide generous fringe benefits. In addition, a high employers' contribution rate is likely to be considered as a generous fringe benefit. In this case, the coefficient of employers' contribution rates has bias caused by unobserved heterogeneity of a worker's ability. The DID approach is a useful way to avoid the bias of unobserved heterogeneity or omitted variables. For this purpose, we will take advantage of a natural experiment offered by the introduction of LTCI in 2000. As we have mentioned earlier, contributions for long-term care are not imposed on anyone under the age of 40. We define the variable LTCI as a dummy variable that takes on the value 1 if the sample is from a year after the introduction of LTCI, and 0 before that, and the variable age 40 as a dummy variable for workers age 40 or older. We estimate a wage equation specified as follows.

$$\ln w_{i,t} = \beta_0 + X_{i,t}\beta + \lambda_1 age 40_{i,t} \times LTCI_t + \lambda_2 age 40_{i,t} + \lambda_3 LTCI_t + \varepsilon_{i,t} \tag{2}$$

Thus, the cross-term of age40 and LTCI is a DID variable, and we can calculate the incidence of employers' contribution from its coefficient λ_1.[2]

However, employers do not have to pay employers' contribution for workers age 40 or older who are non-regular workers. The fact that there are no employers' contributions for LTCI for all age groups of non-regular workers creates a difficulty in applying the DID approach for this group. We therefore perform a DID estimation for regular workers only.

4.2   Data and Descriptive Statistics

The individual wage rate data used in this analysis were obtained from three waves of the Employment Status Survey (1992, 1997, and 2002), released for academic research. The data of contributions to health and long-term care insurance are taken from the Annual Business Report of the National Federation of Health Insurance Societies of the same years.

The annual income, annual worked days, and weekly worked hours are given as categorical data in the Employment Status Survey, and we used their mid-range values to represent each individual.[3] We

---

2   Because workers at age 65 or older pay their contribution for LTCI directly to municipalities, rather than through withholdings from their wages, they will be removed from our samples for wage equations specified in (1) and (2), above.

Chapter 4 An Empirical Analysis of the Incidence of Employers' Contributions to Health Care and Long-Term Care Insurance in Japan **67**

also used the log of hourly wages as our dependent variable. The hourly wages are calculated as follows: hourly wage = individual annual income ÷ (annual worked days × hours worked per week ÷ 5). We constructed dummy variables for female workers, a set of industry dummies for each one in a large classification code (seven categories in our data[4]), four education-level dummies (elementary or junior high school graduate, high school graduate, junior college or technical college graduate, and college or graduate school graduate), and six integrated region dummies (Hokkaido and Tohoku, Kanto, Hokuriku and Tokai, Kinki, Chugoku and Shikoku, and Kyusyu and Okinawa). As the industry classification adopted by the Business Report is more detailed than the one in the Employment Status Survey, we integrated the corresponding industries of

Table 4-1. Names of Variables Used

Name	Description
wage_h	Wage rate per hours (in 10,000 yen)
lwage_h	Log of wage rate
c_rate	Employer's contribution rate (in percent)
female	Female dummy
age	Age (in years)
age2	Square of age
age30	Takes 1 if age is 30 to 65, otherwise 0
age40	Takes 1 if age is 40 to 65, otherwise 0
age50	Takes 1 if age is 50 to 65, otherwise 0
tenure	Number of months worked for the current firm (in months)
tenure2	Square of tenure
income	Annual income (in 10,000 yen)
days_y	Working days in a year (in days)
hours_w	Working hours in a week (in hours)
rgn_1	Region dummy for Hokkaido-Tohoku
rgn_2	Region dummy for Kanto (including Tokyo)
rgn_3	Region dummy for Hokuriku-Tokai (including Nagoya)
rgn_4	Region dummy for Kinki (including Osaka)
rgn_5	Region dummy for Chugoku-Shikoku (including Hiroshima)
rgn_6	Region dummy for Kyusyu-Okinawa (including Fukuoka)
educ_1	Education dummy (elementary school-junior high school)
educ_2	Education dummy (high school)
educ_3	Education dummy (junior college-technical college)
educ_4	Education dummy (college-graduate school)
dyear92	Year dummy for 1992
dyear97	Year dummy for 1997
dyear02 or LTCI	Year dummy for 2002 or year dummy introduced long-term care insurance
LTCI97	Takes 1 if year is from 1997, 0 if year is before 1997

Note: Variable c_rate is the average of all firms in each industry and region. Industry categories are based on the middle classification of industry codes.

---

3   In terms of annual income, the category of 15 million yen and over is set as 15 million yen. In annual days worked, the category of 250 days and over is set as 250 days. In terms of time worked per week, the category of 60 hours and over is set as 60 hours. In terms of working periods, the category of 30 years and over is set as 360 months.

4   (1) Construction; (2) Manufacturing; (3) Electricity, gas, heat, and water supply; (4) Transportation/telecommunications; (5) Wholesale/retail/restaurant; (6) Banking/insurance/real estate; and (7) Service.

the Business Report to match the industries in the middle classification of the Employment Status Survey and took the weighted average of employers' contribution rates, by using the number of employees of industries as the weights. The industry classification that we matched had 35 categories[5] in the middle classification of industry code. The employers' contribution rates are shown as percentages.

The descriptive statistics of regular workers are represented in Table 4-2. Females account for only 24.4% of regular workers, and their average age is 38.2 years. They have worked in the same firm for 14.9 years. During the past year, they worked almost 230 days and 45 hours per week. Their average annual income is 5.708 million yen, which translate into a wage rate of 2,874.5 yen per hour. The combined employers' health care, long-term care, and public pension[6] contribution rate is 13.01%. In terms of educational achievement, the proportion of elementary or junior high school graduates is 6.8%, high school graduates 51.9%, junior college 11.3%, and college or graduate school graduates 29.7%. Although wage rates and employers' contribution rates for each year of our sample are not shown in the table, we

Table 4-2. Descriptive Statistics for Regular Workers

Name	Mean	Standard Deviation	Minimum	Maximum
wage_h	0.2875	0.2191	0.0083	40
c_rate	13.0135	0.9755	11.0752	16.0355
female	0.2442	0.4296	0	1
age	38.1805	11.3295	15	64
age40	0.4647	0.4988	0	1
tenure	14.8661	10.0248	0	30
income	570.8191	301.5686	25	1500
days_y	229.8432	21.3281	25	250
hours_w	45.0364	7.7835	7.5	60
rgn_1	0.0837	0.277	0	1
rgn_2	0.3452	0.4754	0	1
rgn_3	0.2005	0.4003	0	1
rgn_4	0.1528	0.3598	0	1
rgn_5	0.125	0.3307	0	1
rgn_6	0.0928	0.2902	0	1
educ_1	0.0682	0.2522	0	1
educ_2	0.5192	0.4996	0	1
educ_3	0.1132	0.3168	0	1
educ_4	0.2974	0.4571	0	1
dyear92	0.3915	0.4881	0	1
dyear97	0.3579	0.4794	0	1
dyear02	0.2506	0.4334	0	1
Number in sample	137,631			

5　(1) Construction; (2) Food, beverage, and tobacco manufacturing; (3) Textiles; (4) Wood materials, and wood product and furniture manufacturing; (5) Pulp, paper, and paper product manufacturing; (6) Publishing, printing, and related industries; (7) Chemical engineering; (8) Ceramic and rock product manufacturing; (9) Iron and steel; (10) Nonferrous metal manufacturing; (11) Metal product manufacturing; (12) General machinery and tool manufacturing; (13) Electrical machine and tool manufacturing; (14) Transportation machinery and tool manufacturing; (15) Precision machinery and tool manufacturing; (16) Other manufacturing; (17) Electricity, gas, heat, and water supply; (18) Transportation; (19) Railroads; (20) Transportation and warehousing; (21) Telecommunications; (22) Wholesaling; (23) Retailing of drinking and eating; (24) Other retailing; (25) Restaurant; (26) Banking and insurance; (27) Real estate; (28) Service business for individuals; (29) Movies and amusement; (30) Maintenance and fixing; (31) Service business for business office; (32) Medical service; (33) Education; (34) Other professional service; (35) Other service business.

6　We assume that half the public pension taxes have been paid by the employers. Unlike public health insurance, public pension tax is uniform nationally, and there is little incentive for employers to pay more than their statutory share (50% of the tax). We used the tax rates obtained from the Websites of the Ministry of Health, Labor and Welfare (http://www.mhlw.go.jp/english/database/), which are fixed proportions of the employees' standardized monthly payroll.

Chapter 4 An Empirical Analysis of the Incidence of Employers' Contributions to Health Care and Long-Term Care Insurance in Japan

Table 4-3. Descriptive Statistics for Non-Regular Workers

Name	Mean	Standard Deviation	Minimum	Maximum
wage_h	0.123	0.142	0.0083	5.3659
c_rate	12.947	0.8901	11.0752	16.0355
female	0.873	0.333	0	1
age	39.1956	12.4272	15	64
tenure	4.7383	5.0091	0	30
income	111.5635	64.4838	25	1250
days_y	199.9503	49.8913	25	250
hours_w	28.0015	10.9566	7.5	60
rgn_1	0.0876	0.2827	0	1
rgn_2	0.385	0.4866	0	1
rgn_3	0.1603	0.3669	0	1
rgn_4	0.1804	0.3846	0	1
rgn_5	0.0849	0.2788	0	1
rgn_6	0.1018	0.3024	0	1
educ_1	0.1204	0.3255	0	1
educ_2	0.5943	0.491	0	1
educ_3	0.1721	0.3775	0	1
educ_4	0.1107	0.3138	0	1
dyear92	0.2771	0.4476	0	1
dyear97	0.3486	0.4766	0	1
dyear02	0.3743	0.4839	0	1
Number in sample	19,114			

describe those values as follows. In terms of the wage rate, it was 2,731 yen per hour in 1992, up to 3,006 yen in 1997, and down to 2,911 yen in 2002. On the other hand, employers' contribution rates were 12.0% in 1992, 13.54% in 1997, and 13.85% in 2002.

In Table 4-3, we present the descriptive statistics of non-regular workers.[7] The large differences between the two types of workers are in gender composition and labor mobility. Non-regular workers consist mostly of females. In fact, 87.3% of non-regular workers are female, and their average age is 39.2 years old, slightly older than regular workers. They worked for the same firm for 4.7 years, or only one-third as long as a regular worker. During the past year, they worked 200 days and 28 hours per week, which is approximately one-half the time of regular workers. Their annual income, however, is only 1.116 million yen, less than a quarter of regular workers', indicating that their wage per hour is 1,230.4 yen or approximately 43% of that of regular workers. They are less educated: the proportion of elementary or junior high school graduates is 12%, high school graduates 59.4%, junior college 17.2%, and college or graduate school graduates 11.1%. Although wage rates for each year of our sample are not shown in the table, we describe those values as follows: Wage rates of non-regular workers were 1,159 yen in 1992, increased to 1,257 yen per hour in 1997, and maintained almost that level (1,258 yen per hour) in 2002.

5 Estimation Results

First, we show the estimation results of the relationship between the wage rate of regular workers and the employers' contributions to health care and LTCI in the standard specifications of Equation (1).

---

7 In the Employment Status Survey of Japan, temporary and contract workers are classified as irregular workers. However, in many cases, employers are required to contribute for the social insurance programs of those employees. Thus, we have eliminated temporary and contract employees from our sample. In our analysis, we consider part-time employees whose working hours are fewer than 40 as irregular workers.

70

If the wage distribution differed across industries, it led to the heteroskedasticity problem. Therefore, we used the adjustment for heteroskedasticity developed by White (1980). The adjusted standard errors are shown as robust standard errors. Furthermore, if the error terms of individual wages correlated within the industry, it led to the clustering problem. Therefore, we used cluster robust estimation proposed by Liang and Zeger (1986) in order to adjust the standard errors due to the problem of clustering. These adjusted standard errors are shown as cluster robust standard errors. In the first estimated equation, or (I) in Table 4-4, we used the log of individual wage rates per hour of regular workers as the dependent variable. In addition, our estimations include the dummy variable based on the large classification of industry code in order to control for productivity differences. Our estimation result with robust standard errors shows that the coefficient of the employers' contribution rate is negative (with a value of -0.0027), but it is not statistically significant in their wage equation. The variables age, tenure, and education level are statistically significant, and their coefficient signs are consistent with the theory of human capital. The wage rate of females is 26.3% lower than that of males. We also estimate the regular workers' wage equation based on cluster standard errors. The result shows that the employer contribution rate is not statistically significant.

The second estimated equation given in Table 4-4, or (II), is the wage equation of non-regular workers. In this wage equation, the employers' contribution rate has a positive sign and is statistically significant for both robust standard errors and cluster robust standard errors. Furthermore, unlike the regular workers, age and tenure variables are not statistically significant in cluster robust standard

Table 4-4. Estimation Results of Wage Equation

lwage_h	Regular Workers (I)			Non-Regular Workers (II)		
	Coefficient	Robust Std. Err.	Cluster Robust Std. Err.	Coefficient	Robust Std. Err.	Cluster Robust Std. Err.
c_rate	−0.0027	0.0022	0.0309	0.0252	0.011**	0.0047***
age	0.0376	0.0011***	0.0076***	−0.0043	0.0025*	0.0037
age2	−0.0003	0***	0.0001***	0.0001	0*	0
female	−0.2631	0.003***	0.0271***	−0.1308	0.0155***	0.0697+
tenure	0.0326	0.0007***	0.009***	−0.0007	0.0023	0.0026
tenure2	−0.0002	0***	0.0002	0.0007	0.0001***	0.0003*
educ2	0.219	0.0048***	0.0125***	0.0408	0.0119***	0.0237+
educ3	0.3374	0.0057***	0.0127***	0.1027	0.0153***	0.0367**
educ4	0.4432	0.0051***	0.0126***	0.2907	0.0202***	0.0703***
rgn_2	0.1061	0.0042***	0.011***	0.1747	0.0148***	0.0087***
rgn_3	0.0389	0.0043***	0.0155**	0.0559	0.0155***	0.0194**
rgn_4	0.0819	0.0045***	0.017***	0.0958	0.0157***	0.0156***
rgn_5	−0.004	0.0047	0.0082	0.0146	0.0177	0.0345
rgn_6	−0.0225	0.0051***	0.0136+	−0.0597	0.0169***	0.0256*
dyear97	0.0635	0.0041***	0.0554	0.0388	0.0198**	0.0209+
dyear02	−0.0196	0.0048***	0.0597	0.0307	0.0239	0.0204
cons	−2.7412	0.0339***	0.3567***	−2.565	0.16***	0.0921***
Number in sample	137,631			19,114		
R-squared	0.5691			0.1021		
F value	8970.3			68.04		
Prob > F	0			0		

Note1: Estimations include the dummy variables based on large classification codes. Clustering is based on the large classification of industry codes. ***, **, *, and + indicate that the coefficients differ statistically from 0 at the 1%, 5%, 10%, and 15% significance levels, respectively.

Note2: cons is constant term.

Chapter 4   An Empirical Analysis of the Incidence of Employers' Contributions to Health Care and Long-Term Care Insurance in Japan   **71**

errors. On the other hand, the variable of education level is significant, just as in the case of regular workers. The coefficients of females and education are lower for non-regular workers than for regular workers. Furthermore, the coefficient of the employers' contribution rate is 0.025. This implies that the non-regular workers' wage rate increases by 2.5% when the employers' contribution rate increases by 1 percentage point, thereby implying that the cost savings of the employers' from increasing the number of non-regular workers, who are not covered by occupation-based social insurance, exceeds the productivity loss from hiring them. The increase in employers' contributions leads to an increase in the demand for non-regular workers or the substitution of regular workers with non-regular workers, thereby leading to increases in the wage rates of non-regular workers.

Next, we estimate the wage equations using the male or female worker data only. In general, the labor supply for males is more inelastic than for females. According to the theory of incidence, when the labor supply is inelastic, the incidence for employees becomes large. The estimation results are presented in Table 4-5. In the estimated first equation of Table 4-5, or (III), we show the wage equation for regular male workers. The coefficient of the employers' contribution rate is -0.044, which is statistically significant in the case of robust standard errors. This means that the incidence is 0.44, and half of the employers' social insurance contributions have shifted to the employees in the form of reduced wages. In addition, this value is larger than the estimated result, including the female sample in Table 4-4, and is consistent with the theoretical prediction of incidence. However, in the case of cluster robust standard errors, the coefficient of the employers' contribution rate is not statistically significant. Thus, the

Table 4-5. Estimation Results of Wage Equations by Male or Female

lwage_h	Regular Workers (Male Data Only) (III)			Non-Regular Workers (Female Data Only) (IV)		
	Coefficient	Robust Std. Err.	Cluster Robust Std. Err.	Coefficient	Robust Std. Err.	Cluster Robust Std. Err.
c_rate	−0.0044	0.0023**	0.0248	0.0245	0.0117**	0.0089**
age	0.0664	0.0012***	0.0083***	−0.0034	0.0027	0.0047
age2	−0.0006	0***	0.0001***	0	0	0.0001
tenure	0.0214	0.0008***	0.0036***	0.002	0.0025	0.004
tenure2	−0.0001	0***	0.0001	0.0006	0.0001***	0.0004
educ2	0.216	0.005***	0.0208***	0.0427	0.0125***	0.0279
educ3	0.2707	0.0067***	0.0171***	0.1046	0.016***	0.0412**
educ4	0.4053	0.0053***	0.0167***	0.291	0.0241***	0.0719***
rgn_1				0.0002	0.0179	0.0359
rgn_2	0.0847	0.0047***	0.0128***	0.1612	0.0142***	0.0407***
rgn_3	0.024	0.0049***	0.01**	0.0379	0.0152**	0.0259
rgn_4	0.0589	0.0051***	0.0144***	0.0951	0.0156***	0.0529+
rgn_5	−0.0241	0.0053***	0.0082**			
rgn_6	−0.0388	0.0058***	0.0136***	−0.0564	0.0173***	0.0309+
dyear97	0.0716	0.0044***	0.0514	0.0473	0.0208**	0.0319
dyear02	−0.0187	0.0052***	0.0567	0.0468	0.0256*	0.0356
cons	−3.5194	0.0354***	0.2504***	−2.6841	0.1661***	0.2121***
Number in sample	104,028			16,687		
R-squared	0.539			0.0889		
F value	6066.78			54.2		
Prob > F	0			0		

Note1: Estimations include the dummy variables based on large classification codes. Clustering is based on the large classification of industry codes. ***, **, *, and + indicate that the coefficients differ statistically from 0 at the 1%, 5%, 10%, and 15% significance levels, respectively.
Note2: cons is constant term.

negative correlation between the employer's contribution rate and wage rate is not supported sufficiently from our data. On the other hand, the estimated second equation of Table 4-5, or (IV), shows the wage equation of non-regular workers by using the female sample. We use female non-regular workers because there were only a few males in the sample of non-regular workers. The estimation results for non-regular female workers show that the coefficient of the employers' contribution rate is positive and statistically significant in both robust standard errors and cluster robust standard errors. This value is almost the same as in Table 4-4, for estimated equation (II).

Finally, we perform a robustness check for non-regular workers. As previously mentioned, if workers have an unobserved heterogeneity, such as worker's ability, OLS estimation of Equation (1) will have a bias. DID estimation is used to avoid such a bias and we perform this estimation for regular workers in the next section. However, as there are no employers' contributions for LTCI for all age groups in the case of non-regular workers, it is difficult to apply the DID approach to them. We restricted our sample to non-regular workers who were at most high school graduates as a robustness check. Most of them were unlikely to go on to higher education or were likely to drop out because of low or poor academic performance. Therefore, this group is considered as having little unobserved ability to affect their wages. We perform OLS estimation in Equation (1) by using the sample of non-regular workers who were at most high school graduates, including both male and female workers. The estimated first equation of Table 4-6, or (V), shows the wage equation of non-regular workers who were at most high school graduates. The estimated second equation of Table 4-6, or (VI), shows the results of the sample of non-regular workers who were at most high school graduates and under the age of 40. Some of the older females

Table 4-6. Robustness Check for Non-Regular Workers

lwage_h	At Most High School Graduates (V)			At Most High School Graduates, and Under 40 (VI)		
	Coefficient	Robust Std. Err.	Cluster Robust Std. Err.	Coefficient	Robust Std. Err.	Cluster Robust Std. Err.
c_rate	0.0346	0.0122***	0.0056***	0.0522	0.0201***	0.0247*
age	0.0034	0.0029	0.0036	0.0017	0.0109	0.0112
age2	0	0	0	0	0.0002	0.0002
female	−0.1790	0.0187***	0.0831*	−0.0925	0.0236***	0.0696
tenure	−0.0014	0.0025	0.0036	−0.0068	0.0057	0.0056
tenure2	0.0007	0.0001***	0.0004+	0.0013	0.0004***	0.0003***
educ2	0.0325	0.0121***	0.0218	0.0305	0.0265	0.0213
rgn_1	−0.0087	0.0182	0.0291			
rgn_2	0.1544	0.0148***	0.0357***	0.1946	0.0242***	0.022***
rgn_3	0.0447	0.0161***	0.0253+	0.0833	0.0263***	0.0067***
rgn_4	0.0986	0.0165***	0.05*	0.1356	0.0274***	0.0332***
rgn_5				0.0317	0.0274	0.0214
rgn_6	−0.0621	0.0178***	0.0307*	−0.0417	0.0271+	0.017**
dyear97	0.0568	0.0215***	0.0188**	0.0223	0.036	0.0274
dyear02	0.0339	0.0266	0.0269	0.0166	0.0378	0.034
cons	−2.7939	0.1794***	0.1277***	−3.1701	0.3171***	0.2405***
Number in sample	13,661			5,331		
R-squared	0.0765			0.0441		
F value	43.11			12.67		
Prob > F	0			0		

Note1: Estimations include the dummy variables based on large classification codes. Clustering is based on the large classification of industry codes. ***, **, *, and + indicate that the coefficients differ statistically from 0 at the 1%, 5%, 10%, and 15% significance levels, respectively.

Note2: cons is constant term.

were not likely to consider higher education owing to marriage but not owing to poor academic performance. Thus, we estimate the wage equation of non-regular workers excluding workers age 40 and older. Results show that the employers' contribution rates in the first and second equations of Table 4-6 have a positive sign and are statistically significant for both the robust standard errors and cluster robust standard error cases. These results support that the effect of employers' contribution on the wage rate of non-regular workers is positive.

Table 4-7 presents the DID estimations. If there is unobserved heterogeneity such as a worker's ability, OLS estimation of equation (1) will have a bias. In such cases, the DID approach will be useful for avoiding such biases of unobserved heterogeneity or omitted variables. We estimate a specification of Equation(2) for regular workers. In the first estimated equation, or (VII) in Table 4-7, the cross-term of the variable age40 and LTCI is expressed as dd, that is, the variable DID. In addition to the variables shown in Table 4-7, all estimations included the industry dummies based on the large classification of industry code. Estimation results in Table 4-7 are based on the cluster robust standard errors. The results show that the coefficient of DID is negative and statistically significant. The coefficient of the variable dd is -0.0433. This implies that the wages of regular workers ages 40-65 decrease by

Table 4-7. Difference in Difference Estimation

lwage_h	(VII)		(VIII)		(IX)		(X)	
	Coefficient	Cluster Robust Std. Err.	Coefficient	Cluster Robust Std. Err.	Coefficient	Cluster Robust Std. Err.	Coefficient	Cluster Robust Std. Err.
dd	−0.0433	0.0182*						
dd30			−0.0358	0.015**				
dd50					−0.0247	0.0117*		
dd97							−0.0194	0.0185
age40	0.0185	0.0111+					0.0221	0.0155
age30			0.0043	0.0094				
age50					0.0499	0.0122***		
LTCI	−0.0029	0.0127	0.0028	0.0135	−0.0202	0.0179		
LTCI97							0.0349	0.0087***
age	0.0363	0.0081***	0.0375	0.008**	0.0419	0.0068***	0.035	0.008***
age2	−0.0003	0.0001**	−0.0003	0.0001**	−0.0004	0.0001***	−0.0003	0.0001**
female	−0.2631	0.0272***	−0.2628	0.027**	−0.2625	0.0272***	−0.2632	0.0277***
tenure	0.0331	0.0092**	0.033	0.0092**	0.0327	0.0091**	0.0337	0.0092**
tenure2	−0.0002	0.0002	−0.0002	0.0002	−0.0002	0.0002	−0.0003	0.0002
educ2	0.2206	0.0125***	0.2198	0.0123***	0.22	0.0123***	0.2155	0.0122***
educ3	0.339	0.0128***	0.3385	0.0126***	0.3377	0.0127***	0.3311	0.012***
educ4	0.4453	0.0126***	0.4441	0.0125***	0.4432	0.0127***	0.4379	0.0124***
rgn_2	0.1068	0.013***	0.1071	0.0129***	0.1072	0.013***	0.1069	0.0125***
rgn_3	0.0394	0.0101***	0.0397	0.01***	0.0399	0.01***	0.0382	0.01***
rgn_4	0.0822	0.0153***	0.0825	0.0152***	0.0826	0.0152***	0.0825	0.0155***
rgn_5	−0.0040	0.0056	−0.0039	0.0057	−0.0036	0.0059	−0.0044	0.0063
rgn_6	−0.0233	0.0147*	−0.0231	0.0146	−0.0229	0.0147**	−0.0232	0.0151
dyear97	0.0595	0.0156***	0.059	0.0158***	0.0588	0.0157***		
cons	−2.7578	0.1214***	−2.7815	0.1257***	−2.8411	0.1039***	−2.7300	0.1175***
Number in sample	137,631		137,631		137,631		137,631	
R-squared	0.5694		0.5693		0.5694		0.5661	

Note1: Estimations include the dummy variables based on large classification codes. Clustering is based on the large classification of industry codes. ***, **, *, and + indicate that the coefficients differ statistically from 0 at the 1%, 5%, 10%, and 15% significance levels, respectively.

Note2: cons is constant term.

approximately 4.3% relative to those of younger workers. On the other hand, the employers' contribution rates for LTCI in our sample of 2002 were around 0.5%. The magnitude of this estimated incidence is very large relative to previous studies. The results of the other variables are as follows: The variable age40, which take the value of 1 when the worker is over 40 and 0 otherwise, is positive and statistically significant at the 15% level. The variable LTCI is a year dummy, which the long-term care insurance system introduced in 2000. Since our samples are for the year 1992, 1997, and 2002, the variable LTCI corresponds to the year dummy 2002. The variable LTCI has a negative sign and is not statistically significant. The other variables are almost the same as in the first equation in Table 4-4.

The second, third, and fourth equations in Table 4-7, or (VIII), (IX) and (X) in the table, have been estimated to check for robustness in the DID estimations. After 2000, LTCI premiums have been imposed on those aged over 40. Therefore, being over the age of 40 and after 2000 is key in the DID variable. On the other hand, we create the variable age30, which takes the value of 1 if the age is over 30 and 0 otherwise, and the variable age 50, which takes the value of 1 if the age is over 50 and 0 otherwise. In addition, we create the variable dd30 and dd50 as cross-term variables of age 30 and LTCI and age 50 and LTCI, respectively. If the variable dd30 and dd50 are not significant or the variables' impacts are less in comparison with variable dd, age 40 is important. Furthermore, we create the variable LTCI97, which takes the value of 1 if the sample years are 1997 and 2002 and 0 if the sample year is 1992. The variable dd97 is made as the cross-term variable of age 40 and LTCI97. If this variable is not significant, the year 2000 is important. Thus, we use the variables dd30, dd50, and dd97 for robustness checks. Estimation results in Table 4-7 show that both variables dd30 and dd50 are negative and statistically significant. On the other hand, their coefficients are smaller than that of variable dd. Thus, age 40 is the most influential among ages 30, 40, and 50. Furthermore, dd97 is negative, but it is not statistically significant. From these results, the year dummy 2002 is important, and age 40 is the most influential among ages 30-50. Therefore, these results imply that employers' contributions to LTCI lead to the reduction of wages of regular workers or the incidence of employers' contributions to social insurance.

6 Concluding Remarks

In this paper, we empirically analyzed the incidence of employers' contributions to social insurance programs. Our main concern was the incidence of employers' contributions to health care and long-term care insurance. Unlike our analysis, previous studies that sought empirical evidence of employers' contributions to Japanese social insurance programs did not use micro wage data, and did not investigate the effect of social insurance programs on the wage rate with a consideration of the possibility of substituting regular workers with non-regular workers. From our estimation results in the standard specification of wage equations, the negative correlation between the employers' contribution and the wage rate of regular workers was not supported sufficiently. On the other hand, the effect of employers' contribution on the wage rate of non-regular workers was positive and statistically significant, even with cluster robust standard errors. From the estimated coefficient, a 1 percentage point increase in employers' contributions leads to a 2.5% increase in the wage rates of non-regular workers. DID estimation results have shown that the year dummy 2002 is an important variable and age over 40 is the most influential with respect to the wage rate of regular workers. These results imply that employers' contributions to LTCI lead to a reduction of the wage rates of regular workers.

In this paper, since our data comprised a cross-section survey, we were unable to analyze the changes in the employment probability of regular and non-regular workers as a result of change in the costs of social insurance for employers. We leave the empirical analysis of this issue as a subject for future research.

Acknowledgments

This paper is part of the academic work related to the Project on Economic Analysis of Intergenerational Issues, funded by the Scientific Grant-in-Aid for Specially Promoted Research from Japan's Ministry of Education, Culture, Sports, Science and Technology (Grant Number 18002001). We have used micro data from the Employment Status Survey provided by Hitotsubashi University, Institute of Economic Research, Research Center for Information, and Statistic of Social Science for our academic research. The authors would like to thank Naozumi Atoda, Chie Hanaoka, Thomas G. Koch, Catherine McLaughin, Lisa Rochaix, Tadashi Sakai, and Sintaro Yamaguchi for their helpful comments. Needless to say, all remaining errors are our own.

References

Anderson, P. M., Meyer, B. D. (2000) "The Effects of the Unemployment Insurance Payroll Tax on Wages, Employment, Claims and Denials" *Journal of Public Economics* 78, pp.81-106.

Baicker, K., Chandra, A. (2006) "The Labor Market Effects of Rising Health Insurance Premiums" *Journal of Labor Economics* 24(3), pp.609-634.

Brittain, J. A. (1971) "The Incidence of Social Security Payroll Taxes" *American Economic Review* 61(1), pp.110-125.

Gruber, J. (1994) "The Incidence of Mandated Maternity Benefits" *American Economic Review* 84(3), pp.622-641.

Gruber, J. (1997) "The Incidence of Payroll Taxation: Evidence from Chile" *Journal of Labor Economics* 15(3, pt. 2), S72-S101.

Gruber, J., Krueger, A. B. (1991) "The Incidence of Mandated Employer-Provided Insurance: Lessons from Workers' Compensation Insurance" in Bradford, D. (ed.). *Tax Policy and the Economy* 5, Cambridge, MA: MIT Press, pp.111-143.

Hamaaki, J., Iwamoto, Y. (2010) "A Reappraisal of The Incidence of Employer Contributions to Social Security in Japan" *Japanese Economic Review* 61(3), pp.427-441.

Holmlund, B. (1983) "Payroll Taxes and Wage Inflation: The Swedish Experience" *Scandinavian Journal of Economics* 85(1), pp.1-15.

Iwamoto, Y., Hamaaki, J. (2006) "On the Incidence of Social Insurance Contributions: An Economic Perspective" *Quarterly of Social Security Research* 42(3), pp.204-218.

Komamura, K., Yamada, A. (2004) "Who Bears the Burden of Social Insurance? Evidence from Japanese Health and Long-Term Care Insurance Data" *Journal of the Japanese and International Economies* 18, pp.565-581.

Liang, K. -Y., Zeger, S. L. (1986) "Longitudinal Data Analysis Using Generalized Linear Model" *Biometrika* 73(1), pp.13-22.

Sakai, T., Kazekami, S. (2007) "Empirical Study on Incidence of Long-Term Care Insurance" *Health Care and Society* 16(3), pp.285-301.

Sommers, B. D. (2005) "Who Really Pays for Health Insurance? The Incidence of Employer-Provided Health Insurance with Sticky Nominal Wages" *International Journal of Health Care Finance and Economics* 5, pp.89-118.

Tachibanaki, T., Yokoyama, Y. (2008) "The Estimation of the Incidence of Employer Contributions to Social Security in Japan" *Japanese Economic Review* 59(1), pp.75-83.

Thurston, N. K. (1997) "Labor Market Effects of Hawaii's Mandatory Employer-Provided Health Insurance" *Industrial and Labor Relations Review* 51(1), pp.117-135.

Vroman, W. (1974) "Employer Payroll Taxes and Money Wage Behaviour" *Applied Economics* 6, pp.189-204.

White, H. (1980) "A Heteroskedasticity-Consistent Covariance Matrix Estimator and a Direct Test for Heteroskedasticity" *Econometrica* 48, pp.817-838.

Chapter 5

Immigration Policy and Sustainability of Social Security in Japan

Naomi Miyazato

1 Introduction

The aging of the population in Japan is the most severe among all developed countries. Before the baby-boomer generation started to retire, Japan's government proposed and implemented many social security reforms. Unfortunately, it is hard to say if those reforms will achieve sustainability of Japan's social security system. There are only two ways for sound financing of social security: decreasing benefit levels or increasing tax revenues. Although analyzing and debating the recovery of the birthrate have often been discussed for increasing tax revenues, immigration policy has barely been investigated, despite the strong implication for the sustainability of social security.

Razin and Sadka (2000) analyzed the effects of immigrants in a dynamic set-up which included a pay-as-you-go system. They showed the positive effect of immigrants. First of all, working-age immigrants make a net contribution to pensioners in the host country. In the next period, these immigrants have retired and receive pensions. The present value of their pensions may outweigh their contributions during the former period. However, their children make a positive contribution which is sufficient to cover the expenses of their parents. Therefore, the burden of the first generation of immigrants is moved forward into the future. As a result, residents in the host country receive a one-shot gain. If immigration is repeated in each period, or the gain is spread out over all the following periods, all the people in the host country could receive gains, in theory.

Borjas (1994) provided an overview of most of the immigration issue: immigration changes the age composition of the population from the point of view of public finance in a positive direction because immigrants are usually of working age when they arrive in the host country. At same time, they have, on average, a shorter period as retirees. Then, they have effects on lowering public old-age-dependent expenditures and pension benefits. On the other hand, immigrants tend to have higher unemployment and lower wage levels. That means immigrants tend to pay less tax and are a larger fiscal burden. And there may be several general equilibrium effects. An increase in labor supply may lower wages relative to capital. Furthermore, the fertility behavior of immigrants is important. In general, fertility rates of average immigrants are higher than that of host country residents. Wage levels of immigrant's children tend to be relatively low.

There are some studies that carry out empirical and numerical calculations on the effects of immigration. Borjas (1994) computed the net government surplus yielded from the cross-section of immigrants currently residing in the U.S. Simon (1984) and Akbari (1989) computed the tax revenues and government expenditures associated with different immigration cohorts. Bonin et al. (2000) and Auerbach and Oreopoulos (1999) analyzed the effects of immigration through partial equilibrium generational accounting approaches for the U.S. and Germany, respectively. Storesletten (2000) builds a simple computable general equilibrium model to examine the effects of various immigration policies for the U.S. He finds that selective immigration policies, involving an increasing inflow of working-age high- and medium-skilled immigrants, can remove the need for future fiscal reform. In contrast, an inflow of immigrants with the age and skills composition of average immigrants cannot induce a long-run budget balance.

There are some studies which concern European countries. Much empirical evidence was surveyed in Coleman and Rowthorn (2004). Bonin et al. (2000) carried out an analysis for Germany using a generational accounting approach. They found that the increase in average-skilled immigrations improved the fiscal condition of Germany, but inflows of high-skilled immigrants will only be able to partially remove the present fiscal imbalance induced by aging. Roodenburg et al. (2003) also used a generational accounting approach and found that the lifetime net contribution of average immigrants is negative in the Netherlands and an increase in immigration rates would contribute to the sustainability of public finances. Storesletten (2003) performed a partial equilibrium analysis of fiscal implications of immigration to Sweden. He calculated the net present values of immigration effects and shows that average immigrants are not beneficiaries, but some types, 20- to 30-year-old immigrants, improve fiscal conditions. Schou (2006) performed general equilibrium analyses of fiscal implications for the Danish. He found increased immigration would generally worsen the Danish fiscal sustainability problem.

This paper explores whether an immigration policy could mitigate intergenerational imbalances and achieve sustainability of the social security system in Japan. I apply a dynamic general equilibrium simulation model, which was developed by Auerbach and Kotlikoff (1987), to study the effects of immigration policy. By adopting a dynamic set-up, I'm able to investigate the impact on the financing of social security before and after the retirement of immigrants. In addition, I am able to analyze the effect that their descendants would have on the sustainability of social security. Before retirement, an inflow of working-age immigrants increases tax revenues. When these immigrants retire, this effect is reversed. Their descendants have the same effect.

2   The model

I employ the lifecycle general equilibrium model and make use of the overlapping generation model developed by Auerbach and Kotlikoff (1987). This allows us to rigorously analyze changes in the supply of assets caused by demographic change. The basic structure of the model is explained below.

2.1   Demographic Structure and Immigration Policies

The model's households differ by their dates of birth and their lifetime labor-productivity endowments. Every cohort includes three lifetime-earning groups, each with its own endowment of human capital and pattern of growth in this endowment over its lifetime. The three lifetime-earning groups are the low-skilled group, the average-skilled group, and the high-skilled group, respectively.

I used actual demographic structures to achieve realistic simulation results. In this paper, I analyze the transition path in addition to steady states. Simulation periods are 150 years. Demographic structures from year 0 to year 49 in the simulation correspond to real demography from 1950 to 1999, provided by the Ministry of Public Management, Home Affairs, Posts and Telecommunications. After the 50-year simulation, I used population projections for Japan (2002), estimated by the National Institute of Population and Social Security in Japan from 2000 to 2100. Figure 5-1 shows the total population in Japan from 1950 through to 2100. This figure reaches the top at 2007 and decreases after 2007. Total populations are 127,733,000 at 2007, 121,136,000 at 2025, 100,593,000 at 2050, and 64,137,000 at 2100, respectively. Figure 5-2 shows the ratio of the elderly population. This index is the ratio of people 65 years old and over to the total population. These figures are 28.7% at 2025, 35.7% at 2050, respectively. Figure 5-1 and Figure 5-2 imply large impacts from immigration into Japan.

Although people at 75 years old and over exist in the actual demography, I assume people will live from 21 years old to 75 years old, that is 55 periods, to alleviate computational burdens. The immigrants' skills take on three values; low skilled, average skilled and high skilled. Skill are exogenous and do not change during their lifetime. For simplicity, it is assumed that immigrants have children at 30 years old. The fertility rate of immigrants is assumed to be 1.39. This value is same as that of "Population Projections for Japan" in steady states. It is assumed that skills of immigrants' children are given randomly. Even if

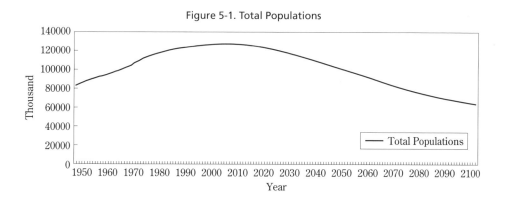

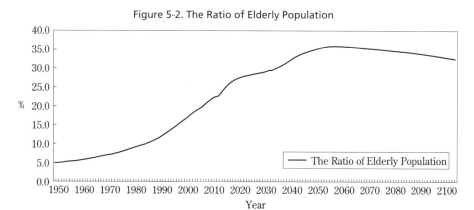

immigrants have high skills, one third of their children become low skill labor and vice versa.

According to OECD (1998), 22,000,000 more immigrants are needed to maintain the ratio of elderly population at preset level in Japan. However, this value is impractical policy because Japan's government has not officially absorbed immigrants yet. So I start to analyze less number of immigrants.

In this paper, I analyze two immigration policies: Case1 is inflow of low-skilled immigrants aged 21 to 30. Case2 is inflow of high-skilled immigrants aged 21 to 30. The number of immigrants at each age is 10,000, so 100,000 more immigrants (inflow) each year. I assume that immigration policies are implemented from 2011 to 2020. Therefore, the total number of immigrants is 1,000,000.

2.2　Households

Households live for 55 periods with certainty, and are divided into three income classes. There are the same numbers of each skill type household among each cohort. Therefore, one third of the cohort is high skill, average skill and low skill, respectively. Each household is assumed to have the same utility function. However, unequal labor endowments create different income levels. It is also assumed that each household appears in the economy as a decision-making unit from the age of 21 and lives to no more than 75 years. Each j-type (j=1,2,3) household who begins economic life at date t chooses perfect-foresight consumption paths (c), leisure paths (l) to maximize a time-separable utility function of the form

$$U_t^j = \frac{1}{1-\frac{1}{\gamma}} \left[\sum_{s=21}^{75} \beta^{s-21} \left(c_{s,t+s-21}^{j}{}^{1-\frac{1}{\rho}} + \alpha l_{s,t+s-21}^{j}{}^{1-\frac{1}{\rho}} \right)^{\frac{1-\frac{1}{\gamma}}{1-\frac{1}{\rho}}} \right] \tag{1}$$

$$j = 1, 2, 3$$

where α is the utility weight on leisure, γ is the intertemporal elasticity of substation in the leisure/ consumption composite, and ρ is the intratemporal elasticity of substitution between consumption and leisure. The term $\beta = 1/(1+\delta)$, where δ is the rate of time preference, is assumed to be the same for all household.

Letting $a^j_{s,t}$ be capital holdings for type j household, of age s, at time t, maximization of (1) is subject to a lifetime budget constraint defined by equation (2)

$$a_{s+1,t+1}^{j} = (1 + (1 - \tau_t^r) r_t) a_{s,t}^{j} + (1 - \tau_t^w - \tau_t^p) w_{s,t}^{j} (E_{s,t}^{j} - l_{s,t}^{j}) + b_{s,t}^{j} - (1 + \tau_t^c) c_{s,t}^{j} \tag{2}$$

$$l_{s,t}^{j} \leq E_{s,t}^{j} \tag{3}$$

and

$$a_{75,t}^{j} \geq 0 \tag{4}$$

where r_t is interest rate, $E^j_{s,t}$ is the time endowment. All taxes are collected at the household level, and the tax system includes the interest income tax τ_t^r, wage income tax τ_t^w, consumption tax τ_t^c, and pension contribution τ_t^p. $b^j_{s,t}$ is public pension benefits. There are no liquidity constraints, so the assets in (2) can be negative.

A household's earnings ability is an exogenous function of age, type, and the level of labor-augmenting technical progress, which grows at a constant rate λ. An efficiency parameter ε^j_s includes all skill differences by age and type. The wage rate for a household of type j and age s is $w^j_{s,t} = \varepsilon^j_s w_t$, where w_t is the real wage at time t. The term ε^j_s increases with age to reflect the accumulation of human capital and the technical progress. I assume that technical progress causes the time endowment of each successive generation to grow at rate λ. Thus, if $E^j_{s,t}$ is the endowment of type j at age s and time t, then $E^j_{s,t} = (1+\lambda)E^j_{s,t-1}$, for all s, t, and j. Because E grows at rate λ from one cohort to the next, technical progress dose not influence underlying trend to w_t.

The age at which households start to receive public pension benefits is RE, the average annual remuneration is H, the replacement ratio is κ. The variable s related to the public pension are represented as follows:

$$b^j_{s,t} = \kappa H^j \qquad (s \geq RE) \tag{5}$$

$$b^j_{s,t} = 0 \qquad (s < 0) \tag{6}$$

$$H = \frac{1}{RE-1} \sum_{s=1}^{RE-1} w_{s,t}{}^j (E^j_{s,t} - l^j_{s,t}) \tag{7}$$

where H represents earned income that is used for calculating the amount of pension benefits. H also reflects the wage rate during the working period.

2.3 The Government

At each time t, the government collects tax revenues and issues debt (D_t). Letting φ^j stand for the fraction of type j households in each generation, the government debt evolves according to:

$$D_{t+1} = (1+r_t)D_t + G_t - (1+n)^t \sum_{j=1}^{3} \varphi^j \times \sum_{s=21}^{75} (1+n)^{-(s-21)} \sum_{k=1}^{K} T^k (B^{j,k}_{s,t}) \tag{8}$$

where G_t is government expenditure. The values of G_t and D_t are held fixed per effective worker throughout the transition path. Any reduction in government outlays resulting from a change in the government's real interest payments is passed on to households in the form of a lower tax rate.

On the other hand, the public pension system is a pay-as-you-go system, and aggregate pension benefits are equal to aggregate pension insurance payments for each period. The budget constraint of public pension is:

$$AB_t = AP_t \tag{9}$$

where AP_t represents the total revenue from the pension insurance contribution. And AB_t represents the total public pension benefit to retired generations. AP_t is defined as follows:

$$AP_t = (1+n)^t \sum_{j=1}^{3} \sum_{s=21}^{RE-1} (1+n)^{-(s-21)} \tau^p_t w^j_{s,t} (E^j_{s,t} - l^j_{s,t}) \tag{10}$$

On the other hand, the total public pension benefit AB_t is defined as follows:

$$AB_t = (1 + n)^t \sum_{j=1}^{3} \sum_{s=RE}^{75} (1 + n)^{-(s-21)} b_{ss,t}^j \tag{11}$$

2.4 Firms and Technology

Aggregate capital (K) and labor (L) equal the respective sums of individual asset and labor supplies as indicated in equation (12) and (13).

$$K_t = (1 + n)^t \sum_{j=1}^{3} \varphi^j \times \sum_{s=RE}^{75} (1 + n)^{-(s-21)} a_{s,t}^j - D_t \tag{12}$$

$$L_t = (1 + n)^t \sum_{j=1}^{3} \varphi^j \times \sum_{s=RE}^{75} (1 + n)^{-(s-21)} \varepsilon_{ss}^j (E_{ss,t}^j - l_{s,t}^j) \tag{13}$$

Output is produced by identical competitive firms using constant-returns-to-scale production technology. In the base case, the aggregate production technology is the standard Cobb-Douglas form:

$$Y_t = AK_t^{\theta} L_t^{1-\theta} \tag{14}$$

where Y_t is aggregate output and θ is capital's share in production. The competitive pretax rate of return to capital at time t is given by the marginal product of capital

$$r_t = \theta A k_t^{\theta - 1} \tag{15}$$

3 Simulation Analysis

The model is solved under perfect foresight by households. The simulation model can be solved using the Gauss-Seidel method.

3.1 Specification of the Parameters

First of all, I have to specify the parameters in order to solve the model. All of the parameters have been set so that the actual value could be reproduced as close as possible. Table 5-1 shows the value of parameters. The value for δ, the rate of time preference is set equal to 0.004 to generate a realistic value for the capita-output ratio in the initial steady state. The values of γ and ρ are those in Auerbach and Kotlikoff (1987). The intertemporal elasticity, γ, is set equal to 0.25. I chose α, the utility function's leisure intensity parameter, such that, on average household devote about 40% of their available time endowment to labor during their working years. Three lifetime-earning groups are the low-skilled group, the

Table 5-1. Parameters

	Definition	Value
α	Utility weight on leisure	1
δ	Rate of time preference	0.004
γ	Intertemporal substitution elasticity	0.25
ρ	intratemporal substitution elasticity	0.8
θ	Capital share	0.25

Chapter 5   Immigration Policy and Sustainability of Social Security in Japan   **83**

average-skilled group, and the high-skilled group. I assume that differences in earnings come from different wage rates. Furthermore, I assume the wage rate of the low-skilled group is 0.8 times that of average-skilled group, and high-skilled group's wage rate is 1.2 times the average-skilled group.

3.2   Simulation Results

Table 5-2, Table 5-3, Table 5-4 provide simulation results for capital stock, consumption and utility levels, etc. Table 5-2 shows the no immigration case results. In the no immigration case, population structures follow Population Projections for Japan (2002). In the steady state, the model generates an interest rate of 6.15%. Capital stock, labor and consumption are 143.24, 20.976, and 30.361, respectively. The social security tax rate is 6.153% and the average utility level is 615474.5. In 20 years from the initial steady state, the interest rate is 6.05. Capital stock is 147.96, labor 21.259, consumption 30.892. The social security tax rate is 6.05%, and the utility level is 625302.6. Capital stock is 150.96, labor 22.224, consumption 29.958 after 60 years. The social security tax rate is 12.265%, and the utility level is 705331.2. Capital stock is 149.72, labor 21.893, consumption 29.643 after 90 years. The social security tax rate is 18.379%, and the utility level is 763595.1. Capital stock is 140.02, labor 21.953, consumption 29.435 after 120 years.

Table 5-2. No Immigration Case

Year	Capital stock	Labor supply	Consumption	Wage rate	Interest rate	Net saving rate	Social security tax	Utility
Initial steady state	143.2406	20.97647	30.36166	1.21016	0.06153	−0.06133	0.01984	615474.5
1	143.2820	20.87485	30.62453	1.21173	0.06260	−0.07292	0.01981	608544.4
20	147.9612	21.25908	30.89256	1.21594	0.06055	−0.05765	0.02172	625302.6
60	150.9697	22.22488	29.95847	1.20857	0.06166	0.00823	0.12265	705331.2
90	149.7292	21.89331	29.64309	1.21062	0.05842	0.00384	0.18379	763595.1
120	140.0278	21.95382	29.43589	1.18970	0.06156	−0.00494	0.17249	721950.8
150	126.3389	20.99816	30.56072	1.17246	0.06431	−0.10039	0.14136	705617.1

Table 5-3. Low-Skilled Immigrants Increasing Case

Year	Capital stock	Labor supply	Consumption	Wage rate	Interest rate	Net saving rate	Social security tax	Utility
Initial steady state	143.2406	20.97647	30.36166	1.21016	0.06153	−0.06133	0.01984	615474.5
1	143.2820	20.87485	30.62453	1.21173	0.06260	−0.07292	0.01981	608544.2
20	147.9613	21.25908	30.89256	1.21594	0.06055	−0.05765	0.02172	625276.4
60	150.8766	22.21942	29.96205	1.20846	0.06168	0.00779	0.12269	713088.1
90	149.2004	21.84664	29.62074	1.21020	0.05848	0.00199	0.17157	759825.6
120	139.5012	21.92810	29.43913	1.18893	0.06168	−0.00687	0.16357	719987.9
150	126.1711	20.99783	30.56065	1.17208	0.06438	−0.10077	0.14175	706029.6

Table 5-4. High-Skilled Immigrants Increasing Case

Year	Capital stock	Labor supply	Consumption	Wage rate	Interest rate	Net saving rate	Social security tax	Utility
Initial steady state	143.2406	20.97647	30.36166	1.21016	0.06153	−0.06133	0.01984	615474.5
1	143.2820	20.87485	30.62453	1.21173	0.06260	−0.07292	0.01981	608543.9
20	147.9614	21.25908	30.89256	1.21594	0.06055	−0.05765	0.02172	625284.2
60	150.8347	22.21637	29.96428	1.20842	0.06169	0.00756	0.12271	694521.4
90	150.0045	21.84761	29.76292	1.21181	0.05825	−0.00066	0.17145	758285.9
120	139.7159	21.92584	29.47571	1.18941	0.06160	−0.00761	0.16301	719725.1
150	126.2124	20.99695	30.56217	1.17219	0.06436	−0.10076	0.14159	705843.0

The social security tax rate is 17.249%, and the utility level is 721950.8.

Table 5-3 shows the effects of low-skilled immigrants increasing. In this case, I assume that age 21 to 30 low-skill immigrant inflow was from 2011 to 2020 (which corresponds to 61 periods to 70 periods in the simulation). The number of immigrants at each age is 10,000. Then 100,000 more immigrants (inflow) each year and the total number of immigrants is 100,000 from 2011 to 2020. Results show that the social security tax is lower than that of the no immigration case in 2040 and 2070 (which corresponds to 90 periods and 120 periods in the simulation). It is 1.22% lower in 2040 and 0.89% lower in 2070.

Table 5-4 shows effects of high-skilled immigrants increasing. Results show that the social security tax is also lower than that of the no immigration case in 2040 and 2070. It is 1.23% lower in 2040 and 0.94% lower in 2070. And consumption is higher than those values in the no immigration case. Moreover, average utility level improves more than that of the no immigration case.

Figure 5-3 is simulated social security taxes. In the no immigration case, the social security tax in 2000 is 8.157% and it reaches 13.57% in 2025, 19.84% in 2045[1]. Both inflows of low-skill immigration and high-skill immigration slightly decrease social security taxes from 2011 to 2020. Figure 5-4 shows difference of social security taxes between the immigration case and the no immigration case. Those differences from 2031 to 2049 widen. Social security tax for the low-skill immigration case is 17.16% and the high-skill immigration case is 17.15% in 2040.On the other hand, the no immigration case is 18.38%. Differences are －1.22% and －1.23%, respectively. Wage profiles are highest around 50 years old. Many immigrants become 50 years old in 2040. Therefore, the burdens on social security per capita are low.

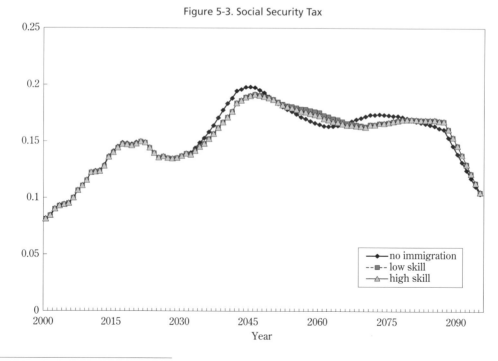

Figure 5-3. Social Security Tax

---

[1] These values are lower than the predicted social security taxes in previous research in Japan. The reason is that the simulation in this paper does not consider people over 75 year old, to reduced computational burdens.

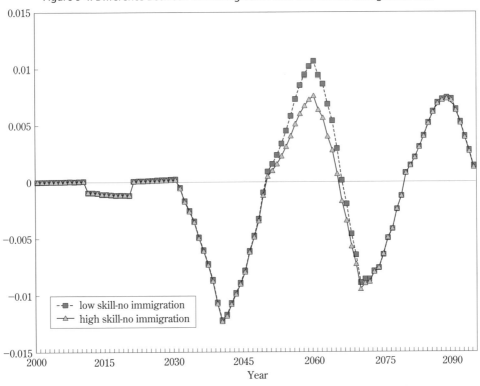

Figure 5-4. Difference Between the Immigration Case and the No Immigration Case

However, these immigrants start to retire around 2045. Social security taxes of the immigration case exceed that of the no immigration case from 2050. This situation continues for 15 or 16 years. Differences of social security taxes become negative from 2066 or 2067 again. This is because the immigrants' children reach the age of higher wage profiles at that time. Figure 5-3 and Figure 5-4 show immigration policies have increasing and decreasing effects on social security taxes. The former is due to increasing numbers of working people and the latter is due to increasing numbers of retired people. I calculate total effects on social security taxes as (16).

$$TE = \sum_{t=2011}^{2100} (SST_t^I - SST_t^N) \tag{16}$$

where SST_t^I and SST_t^N are social security taxes of the immigration case and the no immigration case in t year, respectively. Calculation results are -4.272% in the low-skill immigration case and -8.599% in the high-skill immigration case. Therefore, immigration policies, which are both low immigration and high immigration, have decreasing effects on social security taxes in Japan.

Figure 5-5 shows the effects on the net preset value of social security. First of all, I calculate net preset value of social security as (17).

$$NPV_t = \frac{\sum_{s=46}^{55} b_{s,t+s-1}(1+r_t)/\prod_{j=1}^{s}(1+r_{t+j-1})}{\sum_{s=1}^{45} \tau_{t+s-1} w_{s,t+s-1}(E_{s,t+s-1} - l_{s,t+s-1})(1+r_t)/\prod_{j=1}^{s}(1+r_{t+j-1})} \tag{17}$$

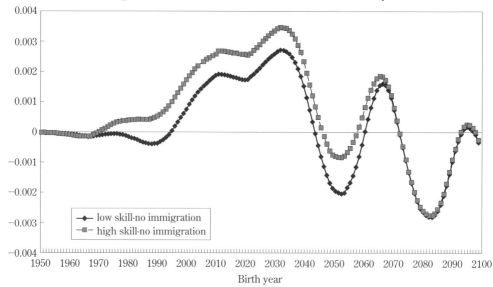

Figure 5-5. Effects on Net Present Values of Social Security

The numerator on the right-hand side of (17) is the net present value of social security benefits, and the denominator on the right-hand side of (17) is the net present value of social security payments. Next I calculate the difference in *NPV* between the immigration case and the no immigration case for each generation. Figure 5-5 shows these results. The horizontal axis represents the birth year. There are some generations whose differences of *NPV* are negative. The reason is that social security taxes of the immigration case exceed that of the no immigration case from 2050 to 2065 and from 2080 to 2095.

4 Concluding Remarks

I analyzed the effects of immigration in Japan by using an over-lapping generation framework. According to the simulation results, both inflow of low-skilled immigrants and high-skilled immigrants decrease social security taxes from 2011 to 2020, from 2031 to 2049, and so on. However, there are some periods where the social security taxes for the immigration case are higher than that of the no immigration case. This is because the number of retired people increases. I calculated the total effects of social security taxes according to (16). Calculation results are −4.272% in the low-skilled immigration case and −8.599% in the high-skilled immigration case. Therefore, immigration policies, which are both low-skilled immigration and high-skilled immigration, have overall decreasing effects on social security taxes. In addition, I calculated the difference of the *NPV* between the immigration case and the no immigration case for each generation according to (17). There are some generations whose differences in *NPV* are negative.

In this paper, I analyzed immigration policies for 100,000 immigrants (inflow) from 2011 to 2020. Therefore, the total number of immigrants is 1,000,000. If immigration policies are implemented continuously after 2020, the results on the differences in *NPV* could change. Analyses of continual immigration policies remain an issue for the future.

References

Akbari, A. H. (1989) "The Benefits of Immigrants to Canada: Evidence on Tax and Public Services" *Canadian Public Policy* 15, pp.424-435.

Auerbach, A. J., Kotlikoff, L. (1987) *Dynamic Fiscal Policy,* New York: Cambridge University Press.

Auerbach, A. J., Oreopoulos, P. (1999) "Analyzing the Fiscal Impact of U.S. Immigration" *American Economic Review* 89, pp.176-180.

Bonin, H., Raffelhüschen, B., Walliser, J. (2000) "Can Immigration Alleviate the Demographic Burden?" *FinanzArchiv* 57, pp.1-21.

Borjas, G. J. (1994) "The Economics of Immigration" *Journal of Economic Literature* 32, pp.1667-1717.

Coleman, D., Rowthorn, R. (2004) "The Economic Effects of Immigration into the United Kingdom" *Population and Development Review* 30, pp.579-624.

OECD (1998) *Trends in International Immigration,* Paris: OECD.

Razin, A., Sadka, E. (2000) "Unskilled Migration: A Burden or a Boon for the Welfare State?" *Scandinavian Journal of Economics* 102, pp.463-479.

Roodenburg, H., Euwals, R., ter Rele, H. (2003) *Immigration and the Dutch Economy,* CPB Netherlands Bureau for Economic Policy Analysis.

Schou, P. (2006) "Immigration, Integration and Fiscal Sustainability" *Journal of Population Economics* 19, pp.671-689.

Simon, J. L. (1984) "Immigrants, Taxes, and Welfare in the United States" *Population and Development Review* 10, pp.55-69.

Storesletten, K. (2000) "Sustaining Fiscal Policy through Immigration" *Journal of Political Economy* 108, pp.300-323.

Storesletten, K. (2003) "Fiscal Implications of Immigration: A Net Present Value Calculation" *Scandinavian Journal of Economics* 105, pp.487-506.

Index

A

accumulation of human capital	81
Aging Policy	3
annual gross income	37
asset accumulations	23

B

basic pension insurance	52
bequests	18

C

Childbearing Incentives	3
cluster robust standard errors	70
Cobb-Douglas form	82
constant-returns-to-scale production technology	
	82
CTC (Child Tax Credit)	33, 37, 41

D

demographic dividend	1, 12
DID (Difference in Difference)	40, 64, 66, 72

E

EITC (Earned Income Tax Credit)	27, 31, 37, 41
elasticity of the demand and supply curves	62
employers' contributions	62, 66
Esping-Andersen	I

F

family support system	5
fertility	45
full-time workers	62
fully funded	56

G

government expenditure	81
government-managed insurance	63

H

health care insurance schemes	64
heteroskedasticity	70
high-skilled immigrants	80, 84

I

immigrants	77
incidence	61
incidence of employers' contributions	74
income effect	39
individual retirement account	47, 50
Intergenerational Equity and Poverty	3
intergenerational relationships	7
intertemporal elasticity of substation	80
inter vivos transfers	18
intratemporal elasticity of substitution	80

L

labor-productivity endowments	78
labor supply	39
lifecycle deficits	17, 19
lifecycle general equilibrium model	78
lifecycle reallocations	17
low-skilled immigrants	80, 84
LTCI (Long-Term Care Insurance)	63, 74

M

medical care programs	7
Moo-Hyun Noh	31
mortality	45
mutual aid associations	63

N

net preset value of social security	85
non-regular workers	29, 61, 65
NTA (National Transfer Accounts)	2-3

O

old-age pensions	7

overlapping generation model	78

P

part-time workers	62
PAYG (Pay-As-You-Go)	54, 56, 58, 81
pension expenditure	57
planned economy	56
population aging	1, 46
public assistance	30
public pension system	47, 81
public social insurance	30
public transfers	23

R

ratio of elderly population	80
real account	58
regional-based insurance programs	65
regular workers	65

S

self-employed	37
self-employed workers	64
social insurance	74
social insurance taxes	61
social pooling	50, 58
social security system	77
social security tax	84-5
society-managed insurance	63
substitution effect	39
sustainability	77

T

TFR	1
The First Demographic Dividend	3
The Second Demographic Dividend	3

U

Urban Residents	48

W

wages	61, 65